Crisis and Hope in American Education

Crisis and Hope in American Education

Robert Ulich

AldineTransaction
A Division of Transaction Publishers
New Brunswick (U.S.A.) and London (U.K.)

New paperback edition 2008
Editor's foreword copyright © 1965 by Transaction Publishers, New Brunswick,
New Jersey. Originally published in 1951 by The Beacon Press.

This book is printed on acid-free paper that meets the American National Standard for Permanence of Paper for Printed Library Materials.

Library of Congress Catalog Number: 2007031601
ISBN: 978-0-202-30984-2
Printed in the United States of America

Library of Congress Cataloging-in-Publication Data

Ulich, Robert, 1890-1977.
   Crisis and hope in American education / Robert Ulich.
       p. cm.
   Originally published: Boston : Beacon Press, c1951.
   Includes bibliographical references and index.
   ISBN 978-0-202-30984-2 (alk. paper)
       1. Education--United States. 2. Education--Philosophy. I. Title.

LA209.2.U4 2007
370.973--dc22

                                                          2007031601

TO

MARY EWEN ULICH

CO-AUTHOR OF THIS BOOK

Editor's Foreword

John Dewey called one of his major works *The Way Out of Educational Confusion.* The choice was an apt one, for it correctly identified the major problem of educational philosophy as one of clarification of problems *and* proposals for solutions. Present trends in the philosophical analysis of educational issues have stressed the former but neglected the latter function. They have also tended to deal with individual and carefully delimited problems of narrow scope and range. In contrast, Robert Ulich has provided here a broad and bold analysis of the causes of educational confusion.

There is a "classical" quality to the work, and this is manifested in several ways. The analysis itself is an attempt to arrive at the *essential* tensions that underlie the establishing of educational policies. These, Ulich says, are the recurring "dilemmas" of education: the relations between quality and equality, the quest for social good and the need for individual freedom, the need for both unity and diversity. The solutions proposed are correspondingly basic and essential ones that always speak to the utterly practical issues confronting the educator, but which at the same time bring to bear on the problem a total theory of knowledge and of society. The highly developed and original point of view that Ulich develops in outline here is this philosophy of *self-transcendence,* a view emphasizing the need for individual freedom and expression to be always in a broader context of social and philosophical meaning. Finally, the work is classical in that it has, in its unabashed treatment of the personality or soul, a decidedly Platonic flavor, emphasizing as it does the neglected legacy that the ancients have provided for us.

Yet that is only half the story, and really the least important half. For Ulich is concerned not with the application of merely modified traditional ideas to a new context but rather with a thorough and fresh analysis of the peculiar problems posed by the need for the nourishing of quality while retaining the essential democratic character of modern America. The America that Ulich examines is one with peculiar national problems engendered by a loss of values through excessive materialism, egalitarian leveling, and the tyranny of the machine. Yet it is also the America which is leader of the free world and responsible for setting a course for it through its own example. The chief means for creating a healthy national body politic and providing a national purpose must be found in enlightened educational policy.

Ulich's prescriptions for education are at once bold and practical. The boldness is perhaps best characterized by his controversial suggestion that the emotional sphere serve as the means of unifying the highly diverse American society. Here we see the influence of modern existentialist theory and its disenchantment with the merely intellectual as a basis for understanding, communication, and meaning. In the sphere of art, music, and drama, we can find a common denominator of experience to bring men together. Again, the applications are highly practical. The school that Ulich proposes is an 'ideal" one, but it is described in considerable detail. Its buildings, facilities, curriculum, and informal programs are designed to provide shared emotional experiences while retaining the need for intellectual differentiation. As an ideal, it is no more unrealistic than *Summerhill*. As a theory of schooling it is considerably more detailed.

The demands for the reprinting of this book indicate that its message is today more urgent than ever. The author maintains that all our efforts to improve the intellectual and moral standards in our high schools will not have the desired effect, nor will they increasingly support the cause of democracy, unless we are bold enough to take radically new steps with regard to the allocation of the right subject matter to the right talent. But there is much danger that we will fail more and more in this most important region of educational policy.

However, we must not give up that precious heritage of the United States, to open secondary education to all who can profit thereby. At present they do not. To combine quality with justice in education is the central purpose of this book.

Reginald D. Archambault
Brown University

Contents

Not an ordinary one is the issue. The United States are destined either to surmount the gorgeous history of feudalism, or else prove the most tremendous failure of time. . . .

For feudalism, caste, the ecclesiastic traditions, though palpably retreating from political institutions, still hold essentially, by their spirit, even in this country, entire possession of the more important fields, indeed the very subsoil, of education, and of social standards and literature. . . .

Our fundamental want today in the United States, with closest, amplest reference to present conditions, and to the future, is of a class, and the clear idea of a class, of native authors, literatuses, far different, far higher in grade than any yet known, sacerdotal, modern. . . .

. . . radiating, begetting appropriate teachers, schools, manners, and, as its grandest result, accomplishing (what neither the schools nor the churches and their clergy have hitherto accomplish'd, and without which this nation will no more stand, permanently, soundly, than a house will stand without a substratum), a religious and moral character beneath the political and productive and intellectual bases of the States. For know you not, dear, earnest reader, that the people of our land may all read and write, and may all possess the right to vote — and yet the main things may be entirely lacking?

from WALT WHITMAN's "Democratic Vistas"

Preface

THIS BOOK IS AN ATTEMPT at evaluating the educational system of the United States from the schools for the young up to the universities and the various forms of adult education. But it is not confined to the evaluation of intellectual achievement. Rather it tries to arrive at some judgment as to whether our schools help people acquire the degree of maturity necessary for participation in the work of a nation which is called upon to assume world responsibilities.

Education, rightly conceived, is the process by which a growing person, according to his individual capacity, is prepared to understand himself, his place in society, his relation to the universe, and to act upon this understanding. A nation, to whatever extent it can afford to do so, should help future generations to strive for such achievements. But although this obligation is generally accepted by the American citizen, its practical requirements are not yet fully understood.

Our various schools are engaged in thousands of curricular experiments and in the writing of reports but, with the exception of some obvious generalities, there is no clarity about important fundamentals and their proper application. The results are an unprincipled adjustment of the schools to pressures from outside, a juggling with subject matter and external requirements, and the comfortable but fallacious belief

xiii

that a longer period of school attendance necessarily produces better education and better men.

I wish to direct the reader's attention in this book to the difference between mere schooling and true education.

If we hold our youth for a longer time in school than was the case in earlier decades, then we have to know what to do with them. Modern industry threatens civilization with the increasing uselessness of our teen-agers in the creative process of social life. Are we perhaps offering our educational institutions primarily as a parking place and as a chance to remove young people from the street, repeating in modern version the old slogan, "Open a school and close a jail"? We have a paradoxical situation in our schools. On the one hand, we fail to utilize the wonderful potential resources of gifted youth. According to all we may guess from statistical data it is overoptimistic to state that about one-fifth of our high school graduates with good intellectual talent continue their education as they should for their own and the nation's advantage. On the other hand, we feed verbal abstractions to young people who do not and cannot profit from them and should have a much more practical — though not at all a narrow — vocational education. Three-fourths of the total amount of school work is still devoted to so-called "academic" subjects, often in diluted form, and only one-fourth to activities of non-verbal character. Thus we waste on two sides at once: we neglect the thinkers and we neglect the doers.

We could phrase the problem also in the following way:

Do we want the public school to create the verbally minded mass man, or do we want it to create the man near to his people, but at the same time secure in his work and his own individuality?

Naturally, the confusion on the secondary school level has extended to the level of higher education. What is a college?

Is it a finishing school? The last refuge of liberal education? A pre-professional or a professional school? Or all these things together?

While asking myself these questions I have constantly kept in mind one moral demand: namely, that one should not criticize without offering constructive proposals. By the admirers of the status quo new proposals are always rejected as "utopian." I shall accept this judgment on my own ideas with equanimity, feeling that I am in good company. For what proposal for human progress, however modest, did not first receive the label of the impossible? Often, indeed, the "utopia" was never fully materialized. Yet a service was done by sharpening men's consciousness and conscience about an important issue.

If in my search for realistic criteria I have sometimes referred to the past and present of European countries it is not because of nostalgic feelings for the old world. I hope I have made it sufficiently clear that I see no salvation in our imitating patterns which have not grown in the American soil and which, rightly or not, fade away even in Europe. But I am convinced that pointing toward the future without knowing the past is the same as pointing into the dark. A nation which refuses to learn by the application of historical and comparative standards will sooner or later have no standards at all.

This book could have been stuffed with innumerable references, controversial discussions, bibliographies, and footnotes. I have abstained from this temptation as far as possible. Everyone acquainted with the great traditions in philosophy and education will immediately sense my gratitude and respect for them. But I wish to emphasize that, in agreement or disagreement, I feel also indebted to such modern writers on education as Boris Bogoslovsky, James B.

Conant, Mark Van Doren, Benjamin Fine, Seymour E. Harris, Sidney Hook, Robert M. Hutchins, Howard M. Jones, Horace Kallen, Ordway Tead, and the authors of such important reports as the Harvard Committee Report on *General Education in a Free Society* and the *Report of the President's Commission on Higher Education.*

For their critical suggestions and revisional remarks I am deeply indebted to three of my colleagues, Dr. S. Willis Rudy, Dr. Cyril G. Sargent, and Mr. John Wendon. I am grateful to Miss Eleanor V. Goldman for her untiring secretarial help.

ROBERT ULICH

Cambridge, Massachusetts

CRISIS AND HOPE
IN AMERICAN EDUCATION

CHAPTER ONE

The Disappointment

FOR HUNDREDS OF YEARS mankind has cherished a great dream: education.

As soon as the early American settlers had built their houses and established civil government, one of the first things they longed for was "to advance Learning, and perpetuate it to Posterity." During the religious wars of the seventeenth century, when cities were ravaged, people tortured, and heretics burned — much as in our times in many nations — the martyrs spoke of the "Path toward Light" and of "Eternal Peace" to be brought about by the education of all children, poor or rich, humble and privileged.

Many attempts were made and many failed. It took wars and revolutions, the new humanism, and the new industrialism, to impose the ideal of public education on an increasingly large number of nations.

A great wave of educational enthusiasm swept over the continents after the First World War. "It must not happen again," people said. "Instead of trusting arms, let us place our faith in enlightenment. Let us send our boys and girls to school not just for six or eight years, but let us open to them the doors of the high schools which so far, in most countries, have been a privilege of the few."

Missionaries of education joined the missionaries of religion; they went to foreign countries, to China, Japan, India, to the Pacific Islands, to Africa. All over the world more and more colleges and universities were built with beautiful libraries and well-equipped laboratories; even the most corrupt governments felt compelled to dazzle their citizens with at least some monumental school buildings. The nation to which most reformers looked as an object of emulation was the United States. Here the majority of children — so they were told — enjoyed the blessings of schooling up to the sixteenth year, and almost half of them even up to the eighteenth year.

Now, after the Second World War, many countries again send their educators to the United States to learn something about schools and schooling. But there is much doubt mixed with the will to profit. Enthusiasm is wavering, both in this and in other countries.

Certainly if we could show the gigantic structure of modern education to the visionaries of earlier centuries they would believe that their dream had come true. But after examining our modern civilization they would, in all likelihood, turn away in disappointment.

Why?

There is no use joining the chorus of those who apparently feel delight in telling that we are the most sinful and rotten generation which ever lived on earth. If our ancestors had had our modern means of destruction, heaven knows how they might have behaved. But it is now a commonplace that we know much more about mastering matter than about mastering ourselves and our social relations. Our present fear is about man himself. The visionaries of old would find torture chambers for whose abolition they had fought. They would see us go through two wars in which more men were killed than in all the other wars during twenty centuries. During the present period of supposed peace more families have been driven from their farms and homes than during any earlier catastrophe that has befallen humankind.

Why has one of our noblest efforts, the improvement of mankind through teaching and learning, brought such disappointing results? Were the great reformers of earlier centuries shortsighted fanatics because they believed that man can be changed through training?

They were neither shortsighted nor fanatics. But they were mistaken in believing that the quality of man can be improved by placing him for many years on an educational island, and by verbal instruction isolated from the total life of the individual and his society. In the meantime disastrous experiences as well as psychiatric and psychological research have taught us that a thin veneer of learning is no protection against the dark powers that lurk in man. Even the best "schooling" without support from deeper sources of motivation does not transform the potential beast in man into a brotherly being. On the contrary, if man's emotional qualities remain without inspiration and direction, all his knowledge and thinking may only create organized barbarism. Yet we still deceive ourselves in believing that the typical classroom is an effective instrument for helping young people to become mature.

The tendency to dramatize the beneficent efforts of schooling has almost become a substitute for religion. From "education" we expect salvation from everything: from sinfulness and race prejudice, from juvenile delinquency and corrupt mayors, from communists and fascists, from dirty streets, and from the atom bomb (which would not have been possible without much education) But our confession of faith in education is frequently nothing other than escape. Whereas political and economic reforms require courage and sacrifice, education costs relatively little; often the sacrifice is on the part of youth who cannot defend themselves against the sins or stupidities of the older generation.

Or the sacrifice may also be on the part of the American teachers. They received, in the year 1948-1949, an average salary of about $2500. That was about the average income level of a factory worker, although the teacher's training is much longer and more costly.[1] Men and women of self-respect who would like to teach our children — and only people with self-respect should teach — are afraid to hire themselves out to communities and states where special oaths may be imposed upon them and where they may be under the continuous censorship of politicians, petty moralists, and those businessmen for whom the mere subscription to a liberal journal is a reason for anathema. Can we wonder that about half of our teachers do not have college degrees?[2] To be sure, the absence of a college degree would be no great disadvantage if it were compensated for by self-education and the wisdom of experience. But self-made men with a resourceful background prefer other outlets for their energy. In the case of teachers, the absence of a higher training indicates generally only a defect.[3]

Wherever institutions arise which provide regular appointments and incomes however small, vested interests create opinions favorable to the enhanced prestige and expansion

---

[1] See "Teachers in the Public Schools," *National Education Association Research Bulletin*, December, 1949, Washington, D.C., National Education Association of the United States.

[2] Special report by Benjamin Fine, *New York Times*, February 22, 1948.

[3] Those who want more information about the financial and social situation of the teaching profession may profitably read Benjamin Fine's *Our Children are Cheated: The Crisis in American Education* (New York, Henry Holt and Co., 1947), though they may disagree in details, and Seymour E. Harris's *How Shall We Pay for Education?* (Approaches to the Economics of Education, New York, Harper and Brothers, 1948). In relation to several topics discussed in this book also the following work by S. E. Harris may be of interest: *The Market for College Graduates* (Cambridge, Harvard University Press, 1949).

of the enterprise. Thus the teachers themselves, both in the secondary schools and universities, have fostered the delusion that the happiness and wisdom of a nation rests primarily on the length of its young citizens' school attendance. But there can be a saturation point in schooling. After this point is passed there will be a continuously diminishing return and finally outright danger and damage. Every businessman knows similar facts about the optimum size of plants and factories. The biologist could point to thousands of examples in nature. Why should it be different with organized and formal education? Have not too many educators been willing to believe that a genuine desire for education on the part of youth was responsible for the general trend toward the extension and prolongation of schooling, rather than such forces as unemployment and the disappearance of the apprenticeship system?

And a fallacious philosophy of education has penetrated many of our schools. A rewarding life is one not merely of so-called freedom and self-assertion, but of discipline, duty, and self-renunciation. But we have coupled education one-sidedly with the idea of satisfaction, going under the name of "self-development." Teachers and parents have become so afraid of creating "frustration" and "inferiority complexes" that, rather than preparing youth for life, they have made it hard for young people to live. Fortunately, we have increasingly become interested in psychological understanding and techniques. Yet the possible advantage has often been lost through the neglect of sound habits of learning and conduct.

Also, to what degree do we renew in our schools the cultural substance on which civilization must live lest it degenerate into training in cleverness? Out of a false regard for the so-called scientific attitude, and partly out of teachers' fear of touching controversial subjects, many of our youth grow up with little knowledge of the great religious and humanistic treasures of mankind. The separation of state and church is a principle that in the course of history has rightly asserted itself against the forces of intolerance and retardation. But none of the great men who in this country fought for this principle, a Jefferson or a Horace Mann, wanted the children of the nation to grow up in a spiritual vacuum where the admiration of a new type of airplane begins to replace reverence for the still greater wonders of man and nature. There is before us the never-ending task of remolding and translating the wisdom of centuries into modern language, and this needs a high degree of interpretative talent and imagination. To what degree is this talent cultivated in our schools of education and our colleges?

We praise the democratic character of the United States school system. There are, indeed, many reasons to be proud of it. Where would this nation be without the powers of unification working in our schools? To a large degree the best in the national ethos of America has been formed by its public schools. And this merit is so great that one might sometimes forget their all too obvious weaknesses with respect to scholastic achievement and intellectual discipline.

But sometimes it seems as if wealth and victory, though certainly more desired, were as hard to live with as defeat. For success easily prevents a people from self-examination and encourages the sort of nationalism which always and everywhere claims to speak in the interest of the nation, but actually undermines its strength. Do we sufficiently realize how much we still have to do in order to live up to our democratic professions? Yet we persist in the unwarranted belief that the whole world has no other wish than to be made over in the image of the democracy of the United States.

Incapable of achieving a deeper synthesis, we have constantly made compromises between the two ideals of democratic education, the ideals of equality and of individuality. In consequence, we have jeopardized both. Some of us confuse democracy with conformity and live in fear of the unusual, the rare, and the dangers of an "elite." Others wish to create the self-reliant and critical individual, the future "leader" and even the "productive rebel." How do these trends fit together? Should it not be possible to create a school system in which both are brought together: the factors which cause men to feel their human community as well as those which strengthen their individuality?

But the source of greatest confusion is perhaps the people who constantly criticize the American school without ever bothering about the social and psychological conditions against which a modern teacher has to work and for the understanding of which he has to be trained — poverty beside wealth, social prejudice and religious intolerance, and parents who in situations of personal failure always blame the teacher and never their child or themselves.

Yet, as already indicated, the school is the institution that keeps the people of the United States more effectively together than her politics, her press, and her churches. If we do not dare examine our school system anew, try to understand its principles and at the same time adjust it to new conditions, we may lose the firmest stronghold in the never-ending battle of civilization.

I shall conduct this examination with respect to three levels of schooling, that of secondary education, of higher education, and of adult education. Furthermore, because of the importance of this subject for the whole educational system, a chapter will be devoted to the preparation of teachers.

CHAPTER TWO

The Dilemmas of
Modern Secondary Education

NEEDLESS TO SAY, in importance the elementary school ranks second to no other school level. In all likelihood, it is also the one in which during the past forty years most progress has been made with respect to methods of teaching and the psychologically wise treatment of children. Though this development has involved a considerable loss of time for the more intelligent children, the majority, let us hope, may have profited. The secondary or high school level has now become the meeting ground of the most crucial pedagogical and social problems, not only in this country, but everywhere.

1. The "Great Investment"?

During the past fifty years the American secondary school has developed quantitatively as probably no other school system at any time except the Russian school after 1918.

Roughly speaking, around 1870 there were some 80,000 children enrolled in high schools and 60,000 in colleges, whereas by 1940 about 7,000,000 were enrolled in high schools and 1,500,000 in colleges. In addition, more than 1,000,000 were engaged in part-time, vocational, and adult education. Or, to put it differently, in the years from 1870 to the beginning of World War II, enrollment in secondary schools had increased ninety times, and college enrollment had increased twenty-five times, all this as compared with only a trebling of the population. If one speaks with young and middle-aged men and women in the United States, except in certain neglected areas, one generally receives intelligent and decent answers, provided the conversation turns around immediate and observable problems. Though people read large quantities of useless and even pernicious literature, many have good books on their shelves. Even the best sellers — with unfortunate exceptions — betray a "civilized" taste; one cannot expect it to be an exquisite one. Local politics in many places have low standards, but for the most responsible offices of the country honest men have generally been elected. The American citizen is rather helpless in controlling external politics and the machinations of power groups, but this fate he shares with the common man all over the world. The age of political individualism is gone.

The intellectual standards in American secondary schools are often discouraging. But, on the whole, the relationship between teachers and pupils is one of friendliness and understanding, schools are concerned with the happiness of their children and not merely with their learning, and, all defects notwithstanding, educators and laymen alike are concerned with the development of sound and unoppressive methods of teaching. Also, the physical and mental hygiene movement has reached deeply into the schools. To summarize, in contrast to European countries with much higher levels of learning for a relatively few, we graduate from our high schools boys and girls who have not been twisted and mis-educated, but prepared to become citizens endowed with sympathy and love of freedom.

This, indeed, is much. Those to whom it seems to be little should go into the schools of other countries, observe their social and political life, see their fears and their ruins, and then ask themselves in which part of the world they would like their children to grow up.

Of course, this is not alone the merit of the American schools, but of American society. However, the question of today is: since American society itself is in a crisis, to what degree does the school merely follow general social developments and errors? To what degree does it prove capable of setting up a cultural policy which can make of education a helper and adviser of the nation and not just a dependent employee, useful and gleeful as long as business goes well, but dismissed when bankruptcy threatens? Thus we may ask again some already proposed questions.

Do the majority of those who go to school for ten, twelve, fourteen, or eighteen years, do so out of a deep desire for learning? Are they really so charmed by their teachers that they desire to sit at their feet for such a long time? Are their parents really convinced of the blessings of these protracted studies? Or are schools often nothing but media for keeping the children off the street, and is the prolongation of attendance due to one of the many losses of modern society, especially the inevitable loss of the old apprenticeship system? On the father's farm or in the neighbor's workshop, it gave the adolescent practical experience and the feeling of usefulness. Can our schools offer anything similar or equivalent?

Are not many of our girls in school because in the modern mechanized household the mother would not know what to do with them, nor would they know what to do with themselves, except in rural districts? Has not education waxed fat on the misery of our industrial age which does not know how to occupy young people under sixteen or eighteen, who have not yet formed their character and consequently would suffer terribly from the curse of idleness?

Many of our best youth are thus caught in a vicious circle. They are impatient to enter into a life which fulfills their desire for doing something useful and employing their overflowing strength. But we tell them that in order to be of any use they have to continue in school. There we feed them with theories they do not want, and subject them to tests and teachers. When finally they are eighteen most of them seem all too glad to get a routine "job" where there is neither a chance for initiative nor for applying the theories they have learned in school.

If half and more of the applicants for even the most insignificant job can attach a high school diploma to their letters of application, why should the employer inquire about the qualities of one who has no such printed record? But not only for individuals, but also for society as a whole, any mere show of education without a really beneficent effect on character, knowledge, and employability is a terrific waste. It is one of the heaviest taxes in terms of both time and money which can be laid upon a nation. In addition, it is thoroughly undemocratic. First, because it favors passivity and discourages initiative, thus changing a people of doers gradually into a people of non-doers. Second, against its very intention, it turns out to be a plutocratic enterprise. For there is much danger that in the long march toward the distant goal of a satisfactory position, the potentially best candidates, if they have no sufficient financial means, may be defeated by those who have been more careful in the choice of their parents.

Thus the inconsiderate prolongation of school attendance, a tendency which is spreading over the world, is often nothing but a penalizing of the individual student, and of more than doubtful value for the total society.

Let us ask a question which seems simple but is difficult

to answer. How many adolescents can really be helped to maturity by intellectual activities?

Naturally, a person is molded only by such activities as touch the source of energy from which motivation can radiate over his whole being. If a specific kind of intellectual exercise is only peripheral to a person's interest, then it runs down like water on a duck's plumage, even though the logical performance may have been tolerably accurate.

In the strictest sense of the word only those persons really "learn" from, or are totally affected by, advanced mental work, who find in scholarly abstractions not "vague generalities" but a higher degree of concreteness — as concrete, in a sense, as the food they eat and the table they touch. Such persons are not necessarily creative — to use a term much overused in modern education. But when they deal with intellectual subjects they feel *as though* they were creative, just as the actor and the musician feel *as though* they participated in the creation of the art work which they themselves never could produce.

In these intellect-centered people there is also "transfer" from one comparable mental activity to another, because the genuinely active center of a person is a pervasive force and applies itself to everything done with love and devotion. To the intellect-centered people also, but to them alone, applies the much decried phenomenon of "intellectual discipline," for in their attempt at ordering impressions and ideas into a coherent system they develop a strong feeling for accuracy and honesty. They feel ashamed if they try to escape this inner demand; for them a sloppy and half-baked solution is no solution at all, but an offense.

To this species of *homo sapiens* belongs the boy who in the middle of the night jumps out of his bed because during his sleep his mind has worked on a mathematical problem —

and now the solution has come! To it belongs the girl who on a lonely walk cites a poem which has revealed to her a new depth of insight and an unimagined beauty of expression. When such young people grow into adulthood the spiritual element will grow with them and show in their personality ever widening circles of sensitiveness like the annual rings in the structure of a tree.

But how many people are of this kind? One, five, twenty per hundred? We do not know. Intelligence tests serve in this respect only as a negative criterion, because persons on a low intelligence level will not belong to the small per cent, but neither do many persons who rate a high I.Q. from test performances. One thing, however, is certain: even in selected schools and colleges a teacher is glad if he discovers a few in each class. And certainly this encounter between teacher and pupil in the realm of the spirit is one of the most exquisite experiences in the lives of both. Most students in our high schools do not have it at all; and in talks with many teachers one may come to the conclusion that they too have not had it, neither as students nor as instructors.

But certain though it is that no civilization can thrive without a select group of men and women having this kind of experience, it is also true that civilization could not exist without the large majority of practical people for whom "intellectual" pursuits are secondary. In advanced cultures even the practical men cannot live and survive without the tool of reason; but reason is for them a utility rather than an end in itself. On the other hand, the spiritual depth of life is not at all inaccessible to them; they may be as near to God as anyone. Not through thinking, but through religion, or art, or love, or suffering, they approach the Eternal. Or they may sense it in the heat and responsibility of action; whether it be great or little does not matter. What matters is that they have a heart and a will to incorporate themselves into the deeply felt community of men and its purposes.

Thus, instead of complaining that so many children "do not like to learn," we ought to give thanks that they are fashioned in this manner. And we ought not to clumsily spoil their self-reliance through inadequate demands on their theorizing and generalizing capacity. If humankind consisted only of potential professors, civilization would break down before it had begun. Only on the broad base of a hard-working and practical-minded people can the scholar and artist work and live. If a culture has grown so old that man is judged only according to his brain, then exactly those who have the brain ought to warn their fellow men that the pyramid of civilization cannot be built upside down. Unless the base rests on the ground, the whole structure will collapse.

But what do we do with all these practical people? We drive them into a state of artificiality. A hundred years ago, as women, they would have been married, or before that they would have helped in the parents' business and with the numerous family of younger children or nephews and nieces. Today, as a meager comfort for what they are deprived of, they read Shakespeare in school, but at home they prefer detective stories, and with each other they discuss sex psychology. They live on compensatory feelings. And to their contemporaries of the more muscular sex the most exciting events in school life are the football and baseball games.

About 25 per cent of our young people are probably too low in native intelligence to understand the logical operations required after the first eight years of education in American schools. Another 25 per cent may be able to "follow" but, in all likelihood, neither their minds nor their tastes receive any deeper influence or incentive from being in school. In educational circles one can hear the opinion that our present schools are unfitted for one-half of the youth. In 1940 about 60 per cent of all our young people were in high school at the age of sixteen, but only about 40 per cent at eighteen. A considerable number leave school for financial reasons, find more inviting conditions elsewhere, or are discouraged. If such discouragement resulted from the school's insistence on high intellectual standards, it would be justifiable and perhaps necessary, provided there are other educational institutions where the slow learner can profit. But since investigation shows that at certain American high schools young people can receive a diploma who, according to reliable measures, have subnormal intelligence,[1] then one becomes doubtful whether there is really any selection on the basis of intellectual standards. In all likelihood the reason for leaving high school is partly lack of means, but mostly young people give up because the school does not provide for them the life they would like to live.

In other words, the so-called sorting machine which the high school is supposed to be throws out too early a lot of nice little apples which ought to go through the whole process and arrive finally at the "Grade A" basket. On the other hand, it carries with it a great number of fruits which the customers, called society, buy under false pretenses. They think they buy quality products, but on honest inspection they would discover the contrary.

Certainly, there are a number of students who leave before graduation and who should have remained. But a large number of youth after sixteen should have other means of

---

[1] Ruth F. Roland, "*The Moron in High School*, A Study of the Pupil with an I.Q. below 75," Unpublished Doctorate Thesis, 1946, Graduate School of Education, Harvard University, pp. 33 ff.

preparation for life than our typical high school. For they are ill at ease in an environment where the main accent is laid either on activities pertaining primarily to the intellect, or on semi-occupational training from which there is little or no transfer over into their future life.

Not that these young people ought to live and grow without schools, for they need a good deal of education and developed reasoning power. But the fact that each of us needs food, a house, and medical advice does not imply that he has to specialize in agriculture, housing, or medicine. With our continual propaganda for prolonged schooling — without thinking about what kind it shall be — we force many young people to march to a melody they do not like toward a goal they will never reach. This process leads neither toward self-development nor toward a better society.

Warning against "too much education" may, of course, bring us dangerously near to those who, for reactionary reasons, are opposed to better schools for more people. For there never has been any period in education when the owners of social privileges did not paint in dark colors the dangers arising from the better schooling of those "whom the Creator has been pleased to put in a humble position." Apparently in some quarters there may still be the fear that they might compete with the children of those "on whom the Creator has been pleased to put the burden of wealth and influence," and that they might eventually wish to change the state of society. Actually, there can never be too much education, even if it may, and will, make people rebellious against social injustice. But though there can never be too many good schools, there remains the fact that inadequate schools are dangerous. Also, the forces which make a nation great are often outside, and not within, the schools.

Between the end of the seventeenth and the end of the nineteenth centuries England had the worst public school system of all the great Western nations. The Act of Uniformity of 1662, and the Five-Mile Act of 1665, both directed against the dissenters from the Established Church, barred the middle classes from carrying out the amazingly progressive educational programs of the Cromwellian revolution, and even from continuing the kind of schooling they had enjoyed before 1640. Not before 1870 was universal national education demanded by law, and it took at least two decades before it was carried into practice.

Horace Mann, often called the father of the American public school, wrote after a visit in Europe the following lines in his *Seventh Annual Report* (1844) to the Board of Education of the State of Massachusetts:

Arrange the most highly civilized and conspicuous nations of Europe in their due order of procedure, as it regards the education of their people, and the Kingdoms of Prussia and Saxony, together with several of the western and southwestern states of the Germanic Confederation, would undoubtedly stay pre-eminent, both in regard to the quantity and quality of instruction.

England is the only one among the nations of Europe, conspicuous for its civilization and resources, which has not, and never has had, any system for the education of its people. And it is the country where, incomparably beyond any other, the greatest and most appalling social contrasts exist; where, in comparison with the intelligence, wealth, and refinement of what are called the higher classes, there is the most ignorance, poverty, and crime among the lower.

At the end of his description of the Prussian schools, Horace Mann writes:

The question is sometimes asked, why, with a wide-extended and energetic machinery for public instruction the Prussians, as a people, do not rise more rapidly in the scale of civilization. . . .

Horace Mann believed there were several answers. He wrote:

The most potent reason for Prussian backwardness and incompetency is this, when the children come out from the school, they have little use either for the faculties that have been developed, or for the knowledge that has been acquired. Their resources are not brought into demand; their powers are not roused and strengthened by exercise. Our common phrases, "the active duties of life;" "the responsibilities of citizenship;" "the stage, the career of action;" "the obligations to posterity," would be strange-sounding words in a Prussian ear. There, government steps in to take care of the subject almost as much as the subject takes care of his cattle. The subject has no officers to choose, no inquiry into the character or eligibleness of candidates to make, no vote to give. He has no laws to enact or abolish. He has no questions about peace or war, finance, taxes, tariffs, post-office, or internal improvement, to decide or discuss. He is not asked where a road shall be laid, or how a bridge shall be built, although, in one case, he has to perform the labor, and in the other, to supply the materials. His sovereign is born to him. The laws are made for him. In war, his part is not to declare it or to end it, but to fight, and be shot in it, and to pay for it. The tax-gatherer tells him how much he is to pay. The ecclesiastical authority plans a church which he must build; and his spiritual guide, who has been set over him by another, prepares a creed and a confession of faith all ready for his signature. He is directed alike how he must obey his kind, and worship his God. Now, although there is a sleeping ocean in the bosom of every child that is born into the world, yet if no freshening, life-giving breeze ever sweeps across its surface, why should it not repose in dark stagnation forever?

Many of our expensively-educated citizens will understand too well what I mean in saying that when they came from the schools, and entered upon the stage of life, they had a practical education to begin. Though possessed of more lore than they could recite, yet it was of a kind unavailable in mart or counting-room; and they still had the A, B, C, of a business education to commence. What, then, must be the condition of a people, to the great body of whom not even this late necessity ever comes?

As studies in contrast are apt to be, Mann's picture is exaggerated, even for the years of the Prussian reaction. And much of what he says applies to the other European countries of his time as well. But we are here interested in two points.

First: England with its poor school system has developed

steadily toward a relatively sound political and moral life, whereas Germany came under the whip of Hitlerism. In other words, schools alone cannot save a people if other important factors are missing.

Second: in consequence of the fortuitous development of our secondary and tertiary school system, are we not forced to say about a considerable part of our actively minded young people what Horace Mann said of the Prussian subjects: "Their resources are not brought into demand; their powers are not roused and strengthened by exercise"? May not an inadequate school render youth accustomed to a kind of paternalism or, if it has too many women teachers, into a maternalism which fits better into the social system of our European grandmothers than into a progressive democracy?

2. *Education and the Quest for Happiness*

But, one may object, young people have the right to be happy, and therefore they need the guidance and protection of the school. We must keep them away from the cruelty of competition and exploitation; we must not expose them to idleness and criminality.

But do "protection" and "keeping away" alone make a young person really happy? Certainly, on the whole, American children are infinitely happier than children in the war-stricken and devastated areas of Asia and Europe, or young Oliver Twist in Dickens's novel. This, however, is not the merit of the high school, but of the general humanitarian and economic development in this nation. In addition, the misery of Oliver Twist is still not completely a story of the past. A child must not necessarily be in an English workhouse of 1830 to suffer terribly. We have even in the United States many a "black boy" as he is described by Richard Wright.

Furthermore, with respect to normal and healthy young people it is a mistake to believe that security to the point of boredom, and protection to the point of infantilism, really mean a haven of happiness — though it may be for the weaklings in every nation. One needs but observe a typical junior or senior class in an ordinary city high school to see that many of them are not happy. Nor is the teacher, for he, or she, feels that about one-third of the pupils have to be dragged along, instead of moving on their own initiative. He sees a lot of sullen faces and sloppy postures of young men who accustom themselves to a kind of inertia because they would like to use their muscles along with their brains, or who feel frustrated because they sense their manhood, physically and emotionally, but have no outlet for it. Other youths, often among the intelligent, are constantly questioning and analyzing without arriving at poise and balance. More or less unconsciously they realize that the great questions of man are answered only by a combination of acting and thinking, not by listening to irrelevant talks.[2]

One of the causes of the failure of the school, moreover, which hits especially the intellectually or economically underprivileged youth, lies in the fact that learning in school often does not pay. All human beings expect some kind of reward from their activities. It need not necessarily be material, though all human life needs a sound material foundation. But somehow the effort must have a meaning and a purpose, particularly if it is as unpleasant as book learning as now carried on is to a large number of older high school pupils. They cannot see the compensation for all their toil just in more knowledge, or more culture, or in a "liberal education." They want something "concrete."

---

[2] Special reference should be made to the chapter on "War and Delinquency" in Francis E. Merrill's book *Social Problems on the Home Front, A Study of Wartime Influences* (New York, Harper and Brothers, 1948).

For the gifted equally there is in education a utilitarian factor, and rightly so. Nobody likes to spend twelve, or sixteen, or even twenty and more years in a state of preparation in order to discover later that society has no adequate use for his learning.

As a result of far-reaching economic changes which affected the Church during the thirteenth and fourteenth centuries, young clerics could not be given the expected parishes though they had studied at the universities of Paris and Bologna under great sacrifices. Consequently the unemployed vagrant scholars used their intelligence to hurl the most vitriolic invectives against the Church. Unfortunately, though right in their accusations, they had no constructive program of their own. The socially most dangerous vanguard of the modern revolutions was the academically trained "white collar proletariat" which had arisen as a consequence of school reforms unrelated to the employing capacity of the respective countries. So far this country, with its rich resources, has been able to sustain a certain balance between its college and university graduates and the professional needs, but according to Seymour E. Harris's already quoted book, *How Shall We Pay for Education?*, this balance is in jeopardy. Professor Harris says on page 70 of his book:

With the spread of higher education [largely due to the "remarkable growth in the numbers attending elementary and secondary schools"] numbers entering the favored occupations grow *pari passu;* and rewards, relative and, in a stagnant economy, absolute, decline. With entry into the professions not free, the excess of supply over demand in markets requiring educated men and women becomes even more serious. The crisis in education, which has been highlighted by strikes of teachers, is, then, not merely a question of inflation; it is a much broader question of the supply and demand for educated men and women on the labor market.

Thus we may properly ask the question as to the degree of expected happiness and satisfaction from education not only with respect to the individual and psychological but also the collective and economic point of view. The answer must be that an undeliberate expansion of the present school system may create in this country the same insuperable problems, individually and socially, which, in combination with other factors, have already shaken the social foundations of several European countries and threaten to do so in Asia. To repeat: if we want to have more education, we must at the same time say: "better education" and "better timing of education." This means a new channeling and distribution of talent which can be achieved only through a radical reform of our secondary schools.

3. *Education and the American Melting Pot*

Certainly the American school serves as the most effective melting pot which the United States has at its disposal for merging the different classes and races into democratic unity. But whereas the elementary school still serves this mission to a high degree, the secondary school shows a close relationship between social status and rank in school, much more than is justified by the proven fact that children of high quality tend to rally to each other. There are two reasons for this stratification. Pupils of lower quality tend to gang up against those of higher quality; and the offspring of families with good physical and cultural inheritance have a better chance to populate the upper brackets of school and social life than children of the less privileged group.[3] It is one of the frequent mistakes of well-intended people to think that mere geographical nearness, or just being together in one

---

[3] See Warner, Havighurst, Loeb, *Who Shall be Educated?*, New York, Harper and Brothers, 1944, pp. 74, 80.

room, automatically improves human relations. As we shall see later on, there can be such improvement, but only if the young people assembled have a common purpose in which all are able to co-operate with a feeling of self-respect, promise, and profit. But this is exactly the factor which is missing in so many schools. If, without any connecting emotional link, some are quick and others slow, some are bright and others dull, then the school community splits. Fortunately, there can be in life such strange things as co-operative competition and vicariously shared distinction. Neither of these dialectical concepts is contradictory in itself. But if difference in social status and difference in intellectual quality come together and there is no overarching dynamic above all these divisive factors, then a school may be a breeding place for the highhandedness and snobbery of some and the resentment of the rest. And then we have not democratic education but induction into class-mindedness. One only needs to observe older youth in the schoolground in order to envisage the reality in our society of cliques, of ingroups and outgroups, and even of acute tensions from above or below. Not only is the poor child made to feel his parents' poverty, but often also the one or two children from wealthy homes are taught that they do not belong to the demos and may go home weeping.

Here again, it would be wrong to blame the teachers, though they themselves, often without being conscious of it, represent besides the good also all the narrow characteristics of the typical middle class spirit. Their attitudes, their prejudices, and their timidities infiltrate into the classroom, the play yard, and into the families of their pupils. But even if the teachers, by some divine decision, represented the only group in the human race free from partial class consciousness in respect to human problems, they could not make an ideal democracy out of the high school. When children become adolescents society puts them into different boxes of social status, even if they protest against this kind of manhandling.

When foreign scholars come as lecturers to some of the beautiful American colleges, they first breathe with a feeling of relief. Here, finally, is a place remote from the competition and the hustle and bustle of city life, a temple for contemplation and concentration, an asylum for deep and lasting friendship (beyond something to eat). After a while these foreigners discover that if the dirt of jealousy and resentment does not invade the scene from outside, human beings can create it from within.

Why should a simple high school be different?

4. Education and Man's Nature

We often hear that the school ought to be the microcosmos of adult society, by which phrase we generally have in mind the familiarization of youth with the positive qualities of the older generation. But, because habituation leads us to accept custom without questioning, we forget that the school, in a way, is even more unnatural than the society of adults, and this all the more the longer it lasts. All culture is, to a degree, unnatural for it is nurture and not nature. But the school is culture distilled and filled in bottles!

Rightly Rousseau says in the famous preamble to his *Emile:*

All things are good as they come out of the hands of their Creator, but everything degenerates in the hands of man. He compels one soil to nourish the productions of another. He blends and confounds elements, climates, and seasons; he mutilates his dogs, his horses, and his slaves; he defaces, he confounds everything; he delights in deformity and monsters. He is not content with anything in its natural state, not even with his own species. His very offspring must be trained up for him, like a horse in the manège, and be taught to grow after his own fancy, like a tree in his garden.

But just as rightly Rousseau continues: "Without this, matters would be still worse than they are, and our species would not be civilized but by halves." So, we have to have schools.

However, we pay for it. Like Rousseau's, every generation has the duty to ask itself how far it has deviated from the "natural state," and whether it has not already transgressed the boundary line beyond which the "degeneration" connected with all culture becomes greater than the profit.

This is the question we have to ask especially with respect to our emphasis on prolonged schooling. In our attempt to heal the sickness of our civilization through more education, are we not engaged in the contrary pursuit, namely, alienating man from himself rather than helping him to find his own sound solution in the inevitable conflict between nature and nurture?

A problem of this kind, or the "Rousseauist experience," lies at the bottom of "progressive education" as during the past four or five decades it has emerged in the modern countries.

But progressive education has been too much a movement of schoolmasters under the leadership of professors of philosophy and education who believed that man becomes the better the more he is exposed to their influence and has some kind of "experiences." Despite all their mottoes about "learning by doing" and their criticism of the old intellectual school, the progressive educators still believe in the school as in the great miracle.

Furthermore, most leaders of the progressive movement have suffered from too easy optimism. To be sure, the ideal of progress can be the symbol of man's admirable and undestructible faith in his future — of the faith that knows the words "in spite of" and dislikes the word "impossible." This sort of realistic yet militant faith is the very vehicle of civilization. But there is also a self-deceiving hopefulness which simply results from lack of experience and erudite thinking. In contrast to their leader John Dewey, who confessed his indebtedness to such thinkers as Plato or Hegel, certain modern reformers do not deem it worth while to bother about anything which has happened before the twentieth century. They substitute modern "social science" for history and hope that by the process of reading the story of human development in reverse they will turn out better citizens. They are busy decrying political isolationism, but at the same time they fight the teaching of languages which might help the student to learn something about other peoples.

Our progressive teachers talk about psychoanalysis — which ought to tell them something about the abysses in human nature. Yet they cling to their naïve optimism and laugh at our ancestors because they believed in guilt and original sin. Certainly these terms stem from a world view different from ours. But in essence they are much more realistic and reach deeper than the plummets of modern "enlightened" and psychological thought generally do.

In order to escape the dilemma arising from the mixture of antirational Rousseauism, diluted intellectualism, and false optimism, the progressives have become believers in method. For whenever the path toward real action and progress is blocked, the stream of energy tends to spend itself in formalism and the cult of method. Administration then degenerates into bureaucracy, and education into technicalities. Red tape in administration and veneration of method in education are one and the same evil. And the mere fact that somebody professes to use "progressive" methods saves him as little from dogmatism as the adherence to a leftist party prevents a man from being a dogmatist and reactionary inside. In judging our own and other people's conduct we often do not realize that orthodoxy and petrifaction threaten not only the conservative, but anyone who is unwilling to assume a comparative and self-correcting attitude.

This criticism is not intended to deny or belittle the merits of progressive education. In many teachers it has created a new conscience concerning their responsibilities to the child, and a profound devotion to their work, made interesting by awareness of its problems. In addition, the so-called conservative schools, much more than they recognize, have profited from the new experiment by slowly adopting many of its revelations.

Even if progressive education had avoided all the mistakes for which it is criticized, it would have been unable to solve our educational dilemma which even the wisest could not foresee at the beginning of our expansion of secondary education. This is the dilemma: *prolongation of school age is in itself not a blessing, but may even be a curse to civilization unless there goes together with the prolongation a revolutionary rethinking of the total program and a restructuring of the total educational system from the secondary school upwards.*

But this revolutionary step has not been dared, either in the United States or in the European countries which after 1918 believed they were serving the cause of democracy by holding more and more people for a longer time in schools. What they learned were revolutions.

5. *Education and Quality*

Inevitably, a school such as our modern secondary school

working toward the most diverse goals under the most contradictory circumstances must reflect this situation in both its curriculum and its standards.

The growing confusion of the program and standards which occurred with the expansion of the older selective secondary school was already felt at the end of the nineteenth century. This was the case in every country. But what is unique in the United States is the so-called "unit system" about which we will speak more at length in our fourth chapter: "Philosophy of Secondary Education."

With this unit system no conscientious teacher or school administrator is satisfied. Everybody feels that it fosters a primarily quantitative, mechanical, and inorganic aspect of learning, that it has destroyed not only the bad and obsolete, but also the good qualities of the older secondary schools, and that the interchangeability of courses, fostered by this system, promotes an escapist attitude among students and teachers.

Often exactly the student who needs it most is spared the effort of testing his own capacity and the challenge of fighting with a real difficulty in the area of knowledge. Education becomes to him a planless travel rather than a continual discipline and enrichment. He learns "getting by" rather than "getting through"; but later, when life itself will try him out, he will have to pay for his and for his teachers' sins of omission.

Yet, the unit system has grown like dry rot into the house of American education. It cannot be eradicated without major alterations, not only with regard to organization, but also with regard to spirit. Thus, little, if anything, is done.

Paradoxically enough, the same school which gives the student so much freedom with respect to the choice of subjects does so only within a limited framework. It divides the program of study into various sections or divisions which are walled off from one another and give the student little opportunity for many-sided development. How many students in the college preparatory division have still a chance to work with their hands?

In addition, there is little opportunity for personal contact among the students living and learning within the different divisions. Also for this reason it is simply not true that the big American high school is a democratic institution in the sense in which most Americans would understand the term; the truth is quite the contrary. Though we have in this country excellent vocational schools, definitely superior to many a college preparatory division, the enormous importance of a good vocational training, combined with an adequate general education, is not yet sufficiently recognized. Often in our departmentalized high schools the vocational section, attended by the future workers of the nation, is used as the "right" place for pupils unable to succeed in the other sections. Thus there has been spread over the vocational department the odor of inferior social as well as inferior educational status. In many American communities the "industrial" school is more or less the school for problem children. What more can be done to confuse the minds about the dignity of craft and labor?

On the other hand, the college preparatory classes prepare their students much less effectively for the higher schools than did the older humanist institutions. If any proof were still needed of the disintegration of our liberal tradition it would be found in the fact that these classes have no independent name of their own and are just called "college preparatory," in other words, designated as mere means to an end outside themselves. Often an expert teacher is appointed who studies assiduously the "college entrance examinations" and tries to find out the most profitable constellation of subjects for the prospective neophyte in the higher arts, without much regard as to whether the chosen constellation is profitable for the student's own liberal education. In addition, since being in the "college preparatory" group carries social prestige, it has to drag along a considerable number of young people with no other relation to academic studies than the desire for social reputation and a better income.

The deterioration of the academic departments of the high school results in the obligation of the colleges to teach more and more subjects which should be taught on the secondary level. There is an enormous invasion of secondary training into the tertiary level: beginners' courses in the most important modern and ancient languages, in mathematics, the sciences, and in "general education," in order to guarantee at least some common cultural heritage and roundness of basic knowledge. More and more junior colleges are established with the promise of preparing their students in two years for "semi-professional" work, and this is good. But in earlier times this goal was achieved by a mixture of high school education and in-service training. Furthermore, there is the danger that these junior colleges will extend their training and become full-fledged colleges, thus adding still more to the prevalence of the academic-theoretical over the practical concept of life.

Through this whole process of procrastination, an intelligent young person is cheated of at least two years of his life, the nation is taxed for instructional work inefficiently done, and the education of a child into the academic ranks costs so much money that more and more families with a cultural tradition (generally accompanied by a relatively modest income) are afraid of bringing up more than one or two children. In addition: without the fault of the individual employer, who cannot escape the laws inherent in modern mechanized industry, our big plants make less and less use of young people. Thus their initiative is increasingly spent in examinations (if not in wars), and so all modern nations become over-aged.

One cannot wonder that under these circumstances people become concerned with the quality of American education and long for the revival of the older humanist schools.

So let us talk a little more about these older schools with their classical or liberal traditions. They were the cultural expression of an upper-class society united by common convictions about the character of Western civilization; they prepared a selected group of students for the university, and dominated secondary education from the Renaissance up to the second half of the nineteenth century. The society that created and cherished these schools believed in the value of the ancient and Christian legacies; it also believed that nobody should be entitled to assume a responsible position whose thinking had not been disciplined and enriched by the ideas and values inherent in this tradition. The liberal studies, or the *artes liberales*, were not only those for the "free man," the *vir liber*, but they were also supposed to be "liberating." For they acquainted the student with the thoughts and work of thinkers and doers who had led humanity out of a state of superstition and dependency toward a state of rationality. And whatever the ideal academic man was going to do, whether he was to write, to heal, to preach, to rule the country, or to teach others how to rule, in every walk of life he was expected to show the spirit of understanding, comparison, and universality.

Closely connected with this pattern of objective values

was a specific ideal of personality, each nation and period modifying it to a degree, yet all meaning fundamentally the same: a gentleman whose mind and manners, whose reason and instincts, and whose knowledge and taste were harmonized by the intimate acquaintance with a great and formative tradition.

We know from history that the reality of classical education fell far short of the ideal, even with this selected group. It has been the tragic fate of all humanist movements in education to degenerate quickly into imitation, philological antiquarianism, and social aloofness from the *"misera plebs."* For disciples too easily mistake universality of attitude for reading so many books in foreign languages, and "general education" for having crammed in so many subjects. What remains is often nothing but a bleak two-dimensional photograph unrepresentative of the real depth and colorfulness of the intellectual landscape.

The formalism of Latin grammar, the memorizing of Greek irregular verbs, the practicing of mathematics without any reference to its principles and application, all this going on under the control of a stiff schoolmaster with a constantly vibrating pince-nez, and a long-nourished desire to burn the textbooks at the graduation festival — in other words, more a "school for death" than a "school for life" — this is the prevailing memory which many a fine European of the older generation has retained from his "humanist" education. The majority, however, seem to be grateful in spite of all the suffering, and even those who are not, often display unconsciously the culture they have received.

But how can we measure the good and the bad we have derived from educational influences? Every man with imagination and ambition is convinced that his education, however good, has deprived him of a still better education. He gauges the possible against the impossible, and the existent against a utopia. If he has learned languages, he deplores his ignorance in the natural sciences; but how can he judge what he would have become without the languages and more science instead? If he has not learned languages, of course he may miss them, but how can he say what he would have lost without the sciences, and whether the effort would have been worth the price? The more complacent type of people are convinced that what they can make use of must have value, and consequently should be learned by everybody. But this is an arbitrary opinion. If someone has forgotten his languages or mathematics because he has not used them, he says they are useless. "One forgets them so easily." But everything is forgotten that is not used. No study, whether language, or mathematics, or physics, or social science, has the privilege of being remembered clearly and for years in a mind which does not exercise itself. So it is actually impossible even for the most conscientious man to judge the value of his education for himself and others.

Another question: do we *really* forget? Though the content of former learning may have sunk below the threshold of consciousness, the experience once had remains a silent partner with us. In this sense the saying is right that a person's culture is that which remains after he has forgotten what he has learned. But if, despite all submerging, the things past remain the silent partners of our life, then much depends on *what* we have forgotten. It cannot be just everything; rather the more significant, more human, and more humane has been the earlier learning, the richer may be the hidden wells of inspiration under the surface of busy adult life.

If these reflections are true, then the older humanist school with Homer, Plato, Cicero, Horace, Euclid, and the Bible as the spiritual godfathers was certainly a good thing, on the often unfulfilled condition, of course, that the student's way to these authors was not barricaded by fear or boredom and bad teachers. But there were also joy and some excellent teachers in the old humanist instruction. What these men may have lacked in psychological and methodological interest, they compensated for in terms of scholarship, and often real wisdom. They certainly were more learned, and more immersed in their subjects than the majority of modern American teachers.

Out of the humanist college or *lycée* in France, the old public school in England, and the German Gymnasium came a surprisingly large number of the best statesmen, scholars, thinkers, and writers. The humanist reform of the secondary schools under Wilhelm von Humboldt in Prussia, taken up by the other German states, produced the amazing rise of higher learning of that country during the nineteenth century. And whereas Germany in the seventeenth and eighteenth centuries possessed almost no mathematician of rank except Leibniz, in the classical schools of Humboldt, with their neglect of the exact and applied sciences, grew mathematicians such as Gauss, Jacobi, and Weierstrass, and a host of researchers who brought revolutions in science and technology.

Of course, nobody knows how geniuses grow. Certainly it is not due to the school alone, nor to any single factor. But the least that can be said in praise of the older classical institutions is that they did not prevent, but made possible, the rise of such an intellectual elite as we are badly in need of today.

It has also been liberal education which up to the end of the nineteenth century, despite all wars, provided something like an international republic of educated men. In all Western countries they had read the same great books; they knew the main modern languages and could correspond with each other; and the rising demon of nationalism was still subdued by a general awareness of a human community.

When in the Seven Years' War Frederick the Great of Prussia, who had Voltaire as one of his most favored guests and at the same time protected the Jesuits, forced his way into the Saxon city of Leipzig, he asked the then famous poet Gellert to meet him for a friendly conversation. When Napoleon had defeated the German troops in the battle of Jena, he expressed his desire to meet Goethe. Is there today such an island for the spirit amidst waves of international hostility?

Some may say that the old humanist schools were the training centers for an elite without social conscience. It is certainly true that they flowered in times of a hierarchical structure of society; they were used by it and made use of it, as do all schools in all times and under all governments. But who protested against the abuse of their poor fellow men in the most terrible period of industrial exploitation in England: the practical businessmen with their immediate and applied training, or men like Thomas Carlyle and Karl Marx with their classical and philosophical education?

Nevertheless, in the United States the old humanist school is gone. Whether it can survive in Europe the future will show. In the best case it will represent only one of several types of secondary education. The decline of the old humanist school is the inevitable consequence of factors beyond the influence of the educator. Our society is no longer hierarchical and no longer gives that prestige and security to families of moderate means which in earlier times took care of the professions and had their main pride in a cultured life and a liberal education of their children. Our society has changed from a largely authoritarian and contemplative into a primarily experimental value system. Restless modern man is too impatient to wait for the slow emergence of the harmonies which are hidden from the hunters for immediate happiness. Increasingly the gap has widened between the traditional curriculum of the older humanist school and modern public and professional concerns. Finally, the interests of talented youth have become more and more absorbed by the applied sciences which promise a more spectacular career than the older humanities. Whether we have become "happier" by all this "progress," this is another question.

Complacency on our part is dangerous since there are secondary school systems in other countries at least as democratic as the United States in which a sense of quality has been preserved far surpassing even that in our best "college preparatory" schools.

When in the Netherlands a student is graduated from one of the four types of secondary schools which give access to the University, he has a reading knowledge, and often even a fair speaking knowledge, of at least two, but mostly three, modern languages besides his mother tongue. In addition to the modern languages the prospective student of the humanities is required to know Latin and Greek. Similar requirements exist for admission to the universities of the Scandinavian countries and Switzerland. In addition, in all these countries the graduate from a secondary school is often better trained in mathematics and the sciences than the American graduate, particularly in their more modern schools with "only" three or two modern languages.

The result shows in the efficiency of the universities of these countries. The Dutch universities have produced philosophical and philological studies of rare excellence. The

Scandinavian universities, during the past decades, have excelled in the humanities, the sciences, and economics to a degree out of all proportion to their size and means. Certainly it would be unfair to compare the typical American college with the Dutch or Scandinavian institutions of higher learning, because the first aim more toward a general education, while the second are for professional studies and research. There are, however, in the United States many endowed universities with scores of graduate schools. Moreover, the student of a Dutch, Swedish, Danish, or Norwegian university lays value on not being merely a specialist. He attends lectures of general value in addition to his professional work, though his secondary school has already given him a liberal education probably as good as that provided by some American colleges.

If one points out these facts in American scholarly committees, he hears that there is no need for concern. It is indicated that the United States is a big and rich country, that the scholars of other nations have to learn English anyhow (why then should an American bother with foreign languages?), that Germany with its "damned efficiency and technical ingenuity" is "knocked out," and that in the future this country will have sufficient financial, industrial, and political influence to maintain its privileged position.

In addition, one hears that during the war the United States surpassed all other nations in applied fields of research.

These facts are true, but the comfortable conclusions drawn are wrong. Outflanking devastated, tyrannized, and fatigued nations is no surprising deed for the only big country that had available all the physical resources and, in addition, was in the favorable position of drawing largely on the theoretical foundations laid by scholars of other countries, especially those trained in German universities.

But what will happen, should the cradle of Western civilization, Old Europe, gradually succumb to its misery? And to what degree can a country uphold the claim to lead politically, unless it leads also culturally? Is any country ever physically so strong that it may not be confronted with new power constellations which demand more than guns and money, namely wisdom, genuine prestige, and a real understanding of the achievements and ambitions of other peoples of the globe?

The danger of isolation is never so great, and the precipice never so near, as when an institution or a country is at the summit of its power. When reading an American newspaper or magazine of today, those who know European history can easily be reminded of Germany after the victory of 1870. The generals speak; the Herrenvolk complex has apparently crossed the ocean and settled here. People do not even feel the cruel vulgarity and the contradictions in the political vocabulary, with "smashing" as one of the frequent terms of recent years. At the same time there is constant fear, and a terrifying lack of imagination. Wealth may purchase much, but can we buy the depths of thought, the strength of motivation, the learning from suffering, and the spur which comes from the localities where life is harder? Can one "control," or in more honest terms, keep down or destroy, the growing germs of vitality in the less fortunate or subdued areas all over the world? Perhaps this is possible for a while, but in so doing one destroys himself. As the Negro leader Booker T. Washington said: "You can't hold a man down in the ditch without staying down with him."

Surely, "nobody wants to do that." America wants nothing but "the happiness and prosperity of all the peoples of the world," and she cannot understand why there are so many "reds" and "rebels" who refuse to become as happy as Americans are and so urgently wish others also to be. In addition, the United States can pay a sufficiently large number of translators and interpreters to find out what is going on in other countries. Yet, translators and interpreters have little resonance and are like strings without the cello unless they work in a nation with numbers of people sufficiently acquainted with, or at least interested in, the other countries or cultures under discussion. The years before 1914, still more the years between the two World Wars, and even more the general helplessness of present American peace politics, ought to serve as a sufficient warning.

What is the lesson of all this? It is that in the realm of civilization mere power and quantity can never replace quality, just as quality without quantity may also be ineffective. This latter point is, after all, the reason why, in spite of all criticism, we in this country continue to advocate prolonged mass education, although on grounds less frequently acknowledged.

Critical educators in this country, of course, have always been aware of the difference between quantity and quality in our schools. Conservative people have shifted the blame partly to the lack of differentiation in the ordinary American high school and partly to the "progressives" — very unjustly because the conservatives have seen even less than the progressives that our whole educational system suffers from defects much more fundamental than might be corrected by better discipline, or organization, or even by better teachers.

Thus the progressive educators rightly took up the gauntlet and started an eight-year investigation with the purpose of finding out whether there was any difference in college achievement between graduates from more conservative and those from more progressive schools.[4] The result of the inquiry was that it does not make much difference what kind of high school program a student follows, provided he achieves "competence in the essential skills of communication — reading, writing, oral expression — and in the use of quantitative concepts and symbols." The report has thus been considered a victory for the type of schooling which tends to eliminate "college preparatory curricula" and the more academic and difficult subjects connected with it.[5]

Even the so-called "conservative" groups seem to have been somehow impressed by the results of a study which took so much time and cost so much money. But rather than offering the basis for sound and well-directed policy, is not the whole *Eight-Year Study* a stringent indictment of our educational system, and, implicitly, a cry for higher quality? To mention the negative factors first: it implies that the American college — an expensive institution for the education of adult young men and women — offers its wares in so primitive a form that it makes no difference whether the student comes with a harmonized knowledge of foreign languages, of mathematics, and the sciences, or without these. As already indicated, the catalogue of a good-sized college contains so many courses for beginners that the student has a wonderful opportunity to receive good credits for courses which in a well-conceived school system would be

---

[4] *Adventure in American Education*, New York, Harper and Brothers, 1942. See particularly Vol. I, *The Story of the Eight-Year Study*, by Wilfred M. Aiken; and Vol. IV, *Did They Succeed in College?* by D. Chamberlin, Enid S. Chamberlin, N. E. Drought, and W. E. Scott.

[5] See Eunice F. Barnard, "The Eight-Year Study of Progressive School Graduates," in *Progressive Education*, 1943, p. 356; Warner, Havighurst, Loeb, *Who Shall be Educated?*, *The Challenge of Unequal Opportunities*, New York, Harper and Brothers, 1944.

given to a fourteen-year-old. The only requirement seems to be that the eighteen-year-old possesses "skill in the use of the mother tongue, reading, and ability to work hard, and 'reasonable intellectual maturity'" (Aiken, *op. cit.*, p. 12). This is surely a modest requirement for young people after twelve years of training.

Let us, then, use an analogy which a friend suggested. In a room without order, without sense of color and harmony, does it make any difference whether you replace one piece of furniture by a different piece? Or, on a typical gingerbread house does it matter whether you add or take away one gable? Certainly not. So, in the curriculum of a high school or higher school without organic structure, where no subject has really led up to a certain end and height and where the relations between various parts of knowledge are not pointed out, a student may just as well attend this or that course or forget this or that subject. For it really makes no difference.

But in order to show now the positive challenge in the *Eight-Year Study* of the progressives, let us say what it proves in addition to its negative points. It proves that a number of boys trained in a good, progressive institution have as good a chance to succeed in college as a similar group trained according to the traditional curriculum. But the progressive schools in question did not just follow any "wild" and incoherent program. On the contrary, they had a plan pursued by interested students under the guidance of inspired teachers.

In contrast, there is in this country a welter of colleges which follow partly a no longer genuine tradition (not humanist, just "conservative") and partly no plan at all. When a "reasonably" intelligent student, coming from the activizing influence of a good progressive school, or from a good small-town school where he has not lost his natural curiosity and still has some order in his mind, when such a boy is thrown into the college pool, he has a good chance to keep his head above the water. The only thing one wonders at is that it needs a study of eight years to discover this fact, and, still more, that there are educators who seem to interpret the results of the *Eight-Year Study* as a license for a merely negative policy. After all, the *conditio sine qua non* for superior success in college, stated by the *Study*, is something which many high school graduates from college preparatory classes do not achieve, namely "competence in the essential skills of communication — reading, writing, oral expression — and in the use of quantitative concepts and symbols."

Defenders of pseudo-progressive *laissez faire, laissez aller* policy in education ought to ask themselves at least one question. Let us assume that a young person does not go to a college, where they seem to believe he can succeed "anyhow," but into practical life. May it not have a certain effect on his personality and his career whether he has a feeling for rational relationships, for clear and energetic work and thinking, for good literature, and for a foreign language and the culture behind it? Is "success in college" really the only criterion of the education extended to the intelligent youth of this country?

But the individual American teacher is not responsible for the chaos. How can a group of schools resemble anything but a jumble if they are supposed to serve simultaneously the idea of conformity and the idea of differentiation, to serve the intelligent and the slow learner, the academic and the practical-minded person, the willing and the unwilling pupil, the one who feels frustrated because he does not learn enough and the other who feels he is forced to learn too much?[6]

What can we do to get out of this unsatisfactory situation? Ask for the old classical institutions of the elite? Try by hook or crook to introduce something like the modern Dutch secondary school, which represents more or less the pattern along which most continental countries worked before the coming of Hitler?

If so, we would imitate something which, as we said, is praiseworthy as a means of educating a selected group. But, according to democratic European educators themselves, their system is in need of reform with regard to the education of the "common man" for whom, fortunately, we have so much respect in this country. At least, we always say so, though we have not really done much better than the European countries. For in their vocational schools, built upon a rather good elementary system, these countries have given the majority of their youth a training not inferior to that of comparable groups in this country, but shorter in time and combined with practical training experience in an office, a shop, or a factory.

Nevertheless in the European system there is one disadvantage which we do not wish to have here. However good the elementary and vocational training in Europe, it is a dead end or blind alley. Except in a few individual cases it provides no access to the higher studies and thus excludes intelligent youth from the opportunity of vying for the more prominent positions. And whether or not the people of the

---

[6] For a recent discussion of the Eight-Year Study, mainly from the statistical point of view, see Helmer G. Johnson, "Some Comments on the Eight-Year Study" and Paul E. Diederich, "The Eight-Year Study: More Comments," in *School and Society*, No. 1875 (November 25, 1950) and No. 1883 (January 20, 1951).

United States live up to their own expectations, mere imitation of European patterns would mean poisoning the American climate. America needs the American breeze; take it away and it would change everything, not only the climate, but also the man. The solution does not lie in backing out toward the roads of the past, but in hewing courageously a path toward the future.

There remains nothing else for us but to aim with all our strength at the combination of two seeming contrasts with simultaneous avoidance of their potential dangers. One of these contrasts is a school structure which avoids division and differentiation, but involves the danger that there may be no quality in the equality (which would be the end of justice). The other is a school structure which emphasizes the idea of selection, but carries with it the danger that the principle of equality might be disregarded (which would be the end of democracy). *The tension and friction of these contrasts is the essential challenge in the educational situation of democracy. We will never be able to cut the Gordian knot completely, but nothing will prevent us more from approximating the goal than complacency, fear of criticism, and lack of courage.*

The following proposals for the reform of the American high school should be read in this spirit of endeavoring to avoid both horns of the dilemma.

CHAPTER THREE

The School of the Future

A. THEORETICAL CONSIDERATIONS

1. *The Common Ground: the Emotions as the Basis for Character Education*

The difficulty that lies in the task of combining the ideal of equality with the ideal of quality has troubled philosophers and statesmen for centuries. No wonder it bewilders also the educators. Furthermore, in this country with its local control and initiative in the field of education, there was not much possibility for the establishment of systematic principles of organization. The rapid growth of a pushing and rampant nation imposed upon the teachers the task of building a common high school upon the common elementary school, while the other nations reserved their secondary schools for only 1 to 3 per cent of their adolescents. And this growth of the American high school coincided with the disintegration of the old system of apprenticeship in the crafts as well as of religious and humanist traditions in the total culture.

Generally speaking, one may ask whether social institutions which involve the interests of whole populations can grow, or have ever grown, according to carefully deliberated policies. More often than not, contingency and pressure rather than clear design are the masters. But if in building a house we join parts which do not belong together, we will never have a good house.

After the old selective secondary school was replaced by the new high school, what really happened? Answer: an enormous expansion in the number of teachers, administrators, pupils, and buildings. Also, an enormous widening of the program of "studies." But all this change was not accompanied by a corresponding change in the fundamental policy and practice of teaching. Despite a large number of committees, among them the famous Committee of Ten (1893) and the equally well-known Commission on the Reorganization of Secondary Education (1911)[1] which phrased the so-called Seven Cardinal Principles, despite the work of Colonel Parker, Dewey, Kilpatrick, and others, the result was mainly adjustment and compromise. Since the program of the old secondary education would have demanded too much from the average high school boy or girl, the foreign languages became optional or were taken out, easier and more utilitarian subjects were added, and standards were lowered. But at the same time the verbalism and abstract character of the older secondary school — which under selective principles were often productive — were retained in the public high school. About two-thirds of its present offerings are verbal, although it is attended by an overwhelming number of pupils for whom mere words and abstractions have little or no appeal.

In order to escape this confusion arising from the unprincipled attempt to bring under one roof the recalcitrant

---

[1] The work of the various committees is described in J. Paul Leonard, *Developing the Secondary School Curriculum* (New York, Rinehart and Company, 1948, pp. 142 ff).

pair of quality and equality, let us ask one central question.

Which are the spheres where human beings, despite all their individual inequalities, can share the experience of communality, and where is the sphere in which co-operation is difficult, if not impossible? Only after clearing up this central point can we hope to develop a sound design for the modern American high school.

The sphere of human experience where the degree of sharing, and consequently also of community in education, reaches far beyond adolescence and the boundaries of individual cultures is the sphere of our physical activities, natural appetites, and emotions. Newton and Leibniz, who as explorers of intellectual problems were miles above the majority of their fellow citizens, had human bodies with all the common needs for food and shelter. In addition, they all, the philosophers, the craftsmen, and the peasants, needed some joy, love, and laughter, and most of them enjoyed some poetry, rhythm, and music. Many of the minuets danced by Leibniz and his friends in aristocratic circles were but old folk rhythms refined by the composers of his time.

Still another example may show the similarity of men in their affective life. Even the expressive genius of a Shakespeare and Goethe would not have sufficed to explain to their townsfolk the human and artistic problems with which they struggled. Perhaps they themselves would have been disinclined to engage in such a process of rationalization and analysis. But since their poetic genius was capable of expressing the heights and abysses of life in emotionally laden symbols, they were and still are well understood by men infinitely below their level of productivity. Here also lies the reason why the wisdom of the great religious prophets, in contrast to abstract philosophies, can be understood without formal education, and why, to point at the other end of the scale, modern tyrants and demagogues successfully employ all sorts of irrational slogans for their purposes.

These remarks do not imply that there are no qualitative and quantitative dissimilarities in the emotional attitudes of different men. There are. One person inclines toward sublimity, another toward brutality; one is shy, the other bold, one is sensitive, the other callous. Yet we will always understand our fellow men better when we follow them in their basic and normal emotional experiences than when we observe their specialized intellectual activities. There also remains the pregnant fact that — for good or for evil — emotions are contagious. They force their way into the other person; mere words or ideas do not. Why then do we not use the culture of the emotions more than we do as the uniting core in all programs of education?

Let us be clear about one fundamental fact of modern civilization. The abysmal breakdown of our Western culture is not due to lack of intellectual training, as so many people think. The common and average man of today knows much more than his ancestors; this is especially the case with the so-called educated class. The cultural ineffectiveness of all our advanced knowledge results from its dismal failure in procuring the kind of education which produces a strong, balanced, and at the same time morally sensitive character. Modern men are stuffed with all kinds of information coming from school instruction, radio, movies, and television. But they are emotionally destitute and therefore do not know how to bind their knowledge and their emotional life into productive co-operation. These men are as they are, partly as a result of unconducive conditions in their life and work, but partly also because the older agents of emotional culture — church, play, nature, and family — have largely disappeared or have become unappealing, and nothing has been put in their stead. Also, in most of our schools, from the elementary level up to the highest level, there exists such a degree of inspirational pauperism that the feelings live in slum conditions whereas the intellect is overfed.

Around 1930, a traveler could observe the strange results of psychic desiccation at certain semi-religious mass meetings in the western cities of the United States. A woman with all the qualities of an old-fashioned movie star talked from a platform filled with flowers, illuminated by constantly changing lights, with sentimentally mixed colors such as rose and violet preferred. Waves of blurred verbiage and music rolled over the audience and swept it into an ocean of irrational drowsiness. After an hour the staring look of trance appeared in the eyes of the listeners, and a few minutes later men and women suddenly rushed toward the platform, wished to be baptized, confessed their sins, and made vows for the future.

Who, for example, were these men? They were bankers, grocers, farmers, truck drivers, and workmen, physically robust, but emotionally and spiritually starving. Too "enlightened" and "advanced," from their point of view, to go to church, sick of the hellfire sermons or abstract deliberations, perhaps immigrants who had left their home country in disappointment, they had failed to take spiritual root in the country of their choice. Maybe there was some financial success after years of hard struggle, but the wife came from a different background, the children were ashamed of the father's foreign habits, and there was no real friendship. Then, out of mere curiosity, such a man attends a meeting of the new sect; the inner tenseness recedes under the spell of a skillful actress who knows how to generate mass psychosis. All the long-neglected, subconscious yearnings break through the thin shell of painfully learned conventions, and the person revels in what he has abhorred so far, in affective intoxication and superstition.

At such an occasion the traveler between the two World Wars could look deep into the depths of human nature. But he could not foresee that a few years later he would observe a similar phenomenon at the mass meetings of the German Nazis, this time not with a harmless revivalist on the platform, but with one of the greatest diabolic actors in the theater of history.

The man who saw clearly the necessity of embedding the intellect in the matrix of sound emotions was Plato, so often cited by humanist educators, and yet by them so little understood and followed. In the third book of *The Republic* he speaks of the responsibility of artists and craftsmen to provide an environment which avoids "gracelessness and evil rhythm and disharmony, because they are akin to evil speaking and the evil temper. But we must look for those craftsmen who by the happy gift of nature are capable of following the trail of true beauty and grace, that our young men, dwelling as it were in a salubrious region, may receive benefit from all the things about them, whence the influence that emanates from works of beauty may waft itself to eye or ear like a breeze that brings from wholesome places health, and so from earliest childhood insensibly guide them to likeness, to friendship, to harmony with beautiful reason. . . . And is it not for this reason . . . that education in music is most sovereign, because more than anything else rhythm and harmony find their way to the inmost soul and take strongest hold upon it, bringing with them and imparting grace, if one is rightly trained, and otherwise the contrary?"[2]

In reading these lines let us remember that by "music"

---

[2] Plato's *Republic* in Paul Shorey's translation, Book III, the Loeb Classical Library, Cambridge, Harvard University Press, 1930.

Plato means not the isolated art performed in our concert halls of today, but music connected with poetry, choir, dance, and drama, as the universal melodic expression of all that is inherently great and sacred in the tradition of the community.

We no longer have, nor can we revive, the unity of cult and daily life, characteristic of young cultures. Nevertheless, only when there exists an emotional base underneath the political and intellectual activities of a people can a civilization be sure of itself and its future. But we men of the twentieth century go on, in the typical, sterile busyness of our time, establish more and more schools, press more and more youth into the narrow molds of rational theory, and are utterly unaware that we build the whole edifice of culture on shifting sand.

In this way — because of the essential unity of man's inner life — we even fail to produce good thinkers. For the productivity of the intellect does not increase in proportion to the quantity of book knowledge crammed into it. On the contrary, many of the great explorers in thought and science testify that, though they would not have succeeded without thorough training, their new ideas often come after long pauses, as flashes sent into the conscious mind from their powers of imagination and intuition. And these powers, after all, need the continual sustenance from strong emotions.

As is true of every great sin of omission, there are reasons also for the modern neglect of emotional culture. Modern civilization was bound to engage increasingly in the teaching of large groups of young people who in earlier times would never have come in contact with books and newspapers. In the course of this development we have discovered how difficult intellectual learning is for the majority of children; how much endeavor it costs on their part and on the part of their teachers; how much psychological analysis and study it requires to understand the path of nature in the evolution of reason. Thus, we concentrated all our effort on the enterprise of intellectual learning.

In contrast, the so-called "instincts," and the main functions of our affective life, develop more or less accidentally. Every sound human being shows the desire to survive, to protect himself; he laughs; in adolescence he begins to take interest in the other sex: all this comes, as we say, "naturally." A mother who discovers the first symptoms of sexual interest in her adolescent daughter is troubled. But if she failed to discover it, she would be still more troubled. So, say the schoolmen, since the affective life is the expected gift of nature, whereas learning does not emerge spontaneously from the wells of creation, let us leave the emotions to themselves and concentrate on grammar and algebra.

In addition, our schools of education have been swept by a quantitative psychology. This psychology feels uncomfortable in the face of mental phenomena which refuse to be caught in the network of tests and numbers. Yet that stubborn attitude characterizes the deeper areas of emotional life. The typical teacher of psychology of a few years ago would not help his students to profit critically from modern depth psychology, to study human beings as they live with all their joys, sufferings, frustrating quarrels and evitable or inevitable conflicts. He would laugh at the suggestion that he use the great dramatic and novelistic literature for the understanding of the human soul. He has even been taught, and teaches his students, never to use such a word as "soul" or "will" or "intuition" or "guilt," which admonition would be proper if he had clearer concepts for these phenomena suggestive of a deeper reality. But since he has not, he tries to solve such problems by paying no attention to them. The result is a deplorable impoverishment exactly in the spheres of life where a teacher should be the guide and helper of his pupils. In short, there was, and often still is, just no "psyche" in the present instruction in psychology. Much of what students hear in their courses is about fifty years behind modern progress in the understanding of human problems, and miles below the height of wisdom which more than two thousand years ago was developed by the Indians, the Chinese, the Greeks, and the Hebrews. The language and imagination of these great peoples seems to be beyond the understanding of many a "scientifically" or "operationally" trained modern man.

Furthermore, we have the paradoxical situation that a relatively easy system of schooling, such as the American high school, has nevertheless developed exactly the most doubtful features of grading, testing, and measuring. This has come about through American decentralization. Centralized countries have their Ministries of Education, whereas the United States has her test agencies. Sound forms of examinations and of resulting competitions are not necessarily emotionally harmful; they may even be conducive to learning and character development. The whole movement of psychometrics is indeed already a great contribution to the understanding of the human being. But it could be more so if it had not isolated itself from philosophical theories of man. If the main selective criteria in our schools are "true-false" tests and other mechanical devices, the concentration of both the teacher and the child is directed toward extraneous performance or toward a narrow form of instruction which may be the opposite of education in its deeper sense.

The results of this emotional neglect and ignorance are that the spiritual ground of life dries out while we learn, teach, and examine more and more, and that men and women who would have the inspirational energy and talent to teach prefer other fields than education.

There is a greater issue involved. Modern man talks about peace and the new international society. But he fails to cultivate those qualities from which, in addition to intelligent action, we could derive the impetus to feel the unity of humankind and to strive effectively for it. Instead of more and more educated men, coming to the fore and steering the shape of nations, our present civilization produces an increasing number of men with great energy and a certain one-sided intelligence but little insight into the deeper concerns of humanity.

2. The Sphere of Differentiation: the Intellect

To the same degree as we should utilize the unifying qualities of the emotions, we should also utilize the unifying qualities of the intellect. But before entering this field let us emphasize once more the danger of a rigid division of man into one half, the emotional, and the other half, the intellectual. In a whole human being there exists the continual interaction between the affective and the rational qualities. When this interaction and cross-fertilization stops, the emotions block the discriminating, rational, and evaluative qualities of the intellect and degenerate into unbearable sentimentality, unsteadiness, or brutality. (The most cruel is often the most sentimental man, capable of torturing his human fellows but incapable of killing a fly, and easily bursting into tears.) On the other hand, without the affective life working upon the intellect, we have the man who takes pride in barren sophistry and relativism, who lacks in the power of decision, or enjoys one of the most pernicious, because subtle, forms of cruelty, namely the use of logic for the mere purpose of negative criticism and destruction.

In addition, everybody has experienced within himself that intellectual capacity increases when motivated by interest and encouragement, both of which are largely emotional in nature. The adviser sometimes has difficulty in discerning whether a child's love for a specific subject or success in it is the result of genuine capacity or of emotional agitation springing from identification with a beloved teacher. And it is equally true that a fine intellect may remain barren if deprived of proper emotional stimulation.

Yet, though we admit the growing importance of widespread intellectual training in advanced forms of civilization, we contend that the intellect is not the only and perhaps not even the primary means of sympathetic understanding between men and men. The culture of the emotions is just as important. To be sure, all our daily conversations, the work we do, the newspapers we read, the radio announcements we listen to, have some sort of reason and conceptual language as their main instrument. But all this, as far as it is really "understood," moves on a low level.

When in the faculty clubs of our universities the mathematician does not sit with the mathematician, but when professors all are mixed together, their conversations generally descend to an average level. That is why creative scholars and artists are disappointing when in groups. The moment when thinking begins to be a systematic effort related to a specific subject, even the most erudite man can communicate only with a small percentage of his fellow men, simply because he does not know enough about other people's subjects of interest. In addition, his thinking is not sufficiently broad to follow the work and effort of an architect and a philologist, a philosopher and a physician, a chemist and an engineer. Most of us who drive an automobile are dependent on the advice of the mechanic in our repair shop. But emotionally we all share each other's hope for success in his work, for a "decent living," for a good family life, and for the blessings of friendship.

Thus, somewhat exaggeratedly, though not without justification, one could say that the intellect divides, whereas the emotions unite. Love between a man and a woman should not be irrational, yet, the moment it becomes a matter of rational analysis, its power is broken. But this cooling effect of rationality is only one side of the picture; the other is that with the progress of intellectual achievement mankind becomes divided into smaller and smaller groups. Specialists do not talk to the people; they talk only to each other and sometimes leave the tragic impression of talking only to themselves.

When does the separation of the people into specialists begin? The answer is given by the history of education. In all nations with a developed school system the separation of children and the experiments in differentiation begin around the age of ten to twelve. Even in the United States with its so-called single track system there begins in the junior high school the division into departments. Much of this differentiation may have to do with class prejudices, but since we find it in such early educational writings as Plato's *Republic*, or in Comenius's *Great Didactics*, it must be based on the common experience that at the beginning of adolescence the differences of "ingenua" become increasingly apparent.

What are the practical educational conclusions from this discussion? They are the following. If we want to preserve in our high schools a generous degree of equality and communality together with quality, we have to use emotional education for the purpose of unification, and we have to differentiate where, after a certain age, people are incurably different: in the sphere of the intellect.

At the same emphasis on the proper cultivation of our emotional life — not in contrast to, but in harmony with reason — one arrives also from another angle.

In his excellent book *The Unique Function of Education in American Democracy* (National Education Association, Washington, D. C., 1937 [especially Chapter VI]) the historian Charles A. Beard declares it to be the function of education in the United States: 1. to develop ethical responsibility; 2. to foster the social virtues by example; 3. to provide for the maintenance and improvement of American society; 4. to nourish the free spirit of science; 5. to prepare youth for associational life and activities; 6. to aid in upholding social values; and 7. to face new responsibilities for the education of adults.

All these functions, as any one social function, require a certain intellectual capacity. But why does Mr. Beard believe that they should and could be shared by the whole American people, not just by a few— though a few will certainly do better than the rest? Because the performance of all these functions and obligations on the part of the people depends, first of all, on a sound emotional life, strong enough to direct the intellect, which is ethically neutral, along the right ways toward democracy. Ethical responsibility requires the emotion of sympathy; social virtue presupposes a sense of identification with the excellent; the improvement of society needs hope and courage; freedom of inquiry needs tolerance and curiosity; associational life is impossible without love and comradeship.

Let us now go one step further in our attempt to find a reliable theoretical foundation for the practical organization of a high school in which quality and equality supplement each other.

There are many possible answers to the question of how it comes about that this bundle of drives, desires, passions, and thoughts that we call a human being does not burst under the pressure of conflicting forces working from within and from without. In short, how does it come about that man can become mature? One of the answers is that man needs a purpose that gives to his life meaning, direction, and, consequently, the possibility of concentration and integration. Such purpose always originates when motivations for action coming from outer experience square with a person's inherent desires and capacities. Only if this squaring occurs will a person feel encouraged and happy in his work.

If our schools fail to help a person discover his purpose they fail in almost everything that really matters. Hence, the question of adequate differentiation is not only a school problem; it is a life problem. And there is great danger that our schools are delinquent in this respect. This applies all the more the longer our young people are kept in the narrowness of classrooms where they would not be of their own choice. For it is precisely in the age of late adolescence and early adulthood that a person needs the chance and the frictions by which to discover where he belongs.

Again here the school needs the advice of a psychology which is experimental, but tries at the same time to understand the more comprehensive life conditions and concerns of man.

Since there exists a concurrency between capacity, inclination, and achievement, observers of human personalities have tended to divide humanity into certain types. This tendency is not without danger because it easily leads toward the belief in fixed patterns of personality and to the disregard of

two facts: first, that individual development is much con-
ditioned by circumstances, and second, that well-endowed
persons have a variety of choices and adjustments. We are
not bees or ants, each of which has its native and noninter-
changeable function. For this reason we cannot sharply
divide the religious from the political, the artistic from the
intellectual, and the contemplative from the active type. In
addition, the process of grouping human personalities into
specific types cannot be strictly objective but depends largely
on the interest and purpose of the divider and on the culture
in which he lives.

On the other hand, some kind of classification of human
beings in the light of a specific purpose is inevitable. Irrespective of such delicate psychological problems as innate
abilities, hereditary endowment, and freedom of choice,
some classification forces itself upon us not only for practical
reasons emerging from the division of labor and interests in
our human society, but also from the observation of the inner
development of young people. But in order to prevent mis-
understandings, we had better avoid the rigid term "type"
and speak simply of "groups."

If we apply these ideas to the problem of differentiation in
the high school, we can venture the following classification.

Some few students are primarily interested in intellectual
activities. For them abstractions are not "vague," or "difficult," or "remote from life," as they are for the practical
mind, but rather intensifications and comprehensions of life,
a sort of higher reality, as they were for Plato. If we examine
this group more closely we find that some of them prefer to
deal with the humanities and social problems, whereas others
are fascinated by mathematics and the natural sciences. We
leave the question unanswered whether this preference is
due to an essential difference in native ability, or whether

the fact that some humanists "hate" mathematics and some scientists do not like "the languages" is simply due to adverse conditions in their education. Probably the latter is true. But whatever the answer, the division of the theoretical group into humanists on the one hand and mathematicians and scientists on the other corresponds roughly with the objective conditions. Who knows anyhow whether the needs and divisions of society determine the interests of man, or the interests of man the needs and divisions of society?

Of the third group of talents, let us call them the "executive" group, it is difficult to give an exact definition, first because they represent a more complex psychological picture than the primarily theoretical groups, and second because the scale of their activities covers a wide area in the occupational life of a nation, from the political and organizational leader down to the business clerk. Some of this group may intellectually be equal to the young humanists and scientists. But instead of being attracted by theoretical problems, they are anxious to apply knowledge to practical tasks. They like to organize, to master situations and human relations, or to acquire wealth and influence. Though they may have the "stuff" for the scholar, they do not wish to be one. They have something in addition, a deep urge for social responsibility or for power over affairs or for both.

They are doers. Psychologically speaking, they are primarily extrovertive; philosophically speaking, many of them are the living representatives of the doctrine of "well-understood interest." When a problem is driven beyond the realm of immediacy and utility their astonished and suspicious question is: "What for?" They may "like" poetry and the fine arts, but they are inclined to attribute to art mainly a pleasure function. For the profoundly mystic quality of life they either have no sensitiveness, or do not dare show it to themselves and others. There is danger that this type of talent discovers that one can achieve much quick and external success with an elastic conscience and strong elbows. There is all the more reason to insist on a broad cultural foundation exactly among those whose personal and administrative talents may make them most influential in our competitive life.

So far we have spoken of the more talented youth of the executive group. It contains, however, a large section who will fill the middle and lower brackets of our business employees and our officialdom. These men and women are not creative in the strictest sense of the word; yet, we all depend on their understanding co-operation. So, in their education, let us give them a sense for the totality of the social organism of which they will be a part: of government and law, of production, distribution, and transportation, of finance and accounting. And many of them will see the need for learning a foreign language.

Then we all know of a fourth group of people, whose talent lies in their skill as artisans. Though not primarily intellectual, they are not at all without highly valuable talent. The difference is in kind, not in quality. Many of them are capable of understanding even difficult problems, so long as these come out of a concrete situation. Some of them may be our future sculptors, painters, musicians, and designers. They may be the builders of the subtle apparatuses in our laboratories without which the scholar would be unable to perform his experiments, or they may be the craftsmen on whom the engineer and the surgeon depend.

Society has a much greater obligation to them than that discharged in our modern school system, in spite of all our lip service. Have we really tried to use the talent which some people have in their hands, or their eyes, or their ears,

for developing the person as a whole? Have we really understood that such talent — much more than just being "practical," or "decorative," or "useful" — can be a source of beauty
and satisfaction both for individuals and for the community
as a whole? At the time when art was not yet isolated from
both the crafts and communal life, the old sculptors and
painters must have represented the flower of this skillful
and sensuous type.

Fifth and finally, there are those who have not been
blessed with any highly differentiated talent. They are
"average," or even a little below average. They are fully as
useful and as good citizens as members of the other groups;
as a matter of fact, they keep the wheels of civilization going.
Yet, in the present high school situation youngsters of this
group are fed with stones instead of with the bread they
need. Three factors have caused this situation: first, the
resentment against acknowledging real intellectual differences, resulting from a mistaken sense of equality contradictory to nature and society; second, a soundly reinforced
admiration for book learning despite all pious assertions to
the contrary; third, outright laziness, because it is much
easier and much less expensive to feed the majority of our
high school youngsters with the leftovers from the old theoretical secondary school than to create a practical and
adequate institution for the youth between 14 and 18 who
a hundred years ago would have gone into practical life. It
has always been easier to improvise than to create.

Our obligation to democracy and equality is not, however,
in denying man's inequality with respect to talent. It is to
build a society in which men with minor gifts of the intellect
can feel equality in all their claims for development and a
decent life, can escape exploitation, use their faculties with
a feeling of self-respect, gain the reward they deserve, and

live as citizens who, though not capable of leadership in large affairs or organizations, nevertheless understand whom to follow, how to follow, and when to follow.

Let us now take together the five groups just described, all potentially useful and able to maintain their place in society. (For subnormal children special schools will have to be founded.) During the past fifty years the secondary school systems in most countries have been built somewhat according to these categories, though more or less haphazardly and often with definite class differentiations attached to one or the other group. Also in the bigger American high schools we have similar subdivisions: we have a "college preparatory" division for the prospective humanists; a "scientific" division for the prospective scientists and engineers; we have a "commercial" division, which generally prepares young people for the more clerical work in business; and finally a "vocational" branch for the more skilled manual group.

Yet we all feel that something is wrong about this division, and many of us go around with a bad conscience.

The first reason for dissatisfaction is that this development is much less the result of educational planning than of a fortuitous reaction to new social forces. By keeping all these divisions under the same roof, we try to preserve the ideal of the American democratic and unified school system, whereas, in reality, another design already prevails. The older pattern of the same school for all pupils still exists only in smaller communities. Even there, the development of the "consolidated" high schools proves that the rural districts also wish to have more choice for their children.

The second reason for our dissatisfaction lies in the fact that, despite all "democratic" phraseology, our modern high school divisions are not really on an equal level. Qualitatively and socially they operate on a descending scale from the college preparatory to the vocational department. This is partly inevitable because even the best school cannot escape the prejudices of the surrounding society. Yet by offering equally valuable, though articulated instruction to all its students, our schools could do much to offset the social discriminations which prevail in our communities.

As a result of these discrepancies, the modern college preparatory division represents a gross distortion of the older ideal of humanist education, which was not just "preparatory" but had a title and aim in its own right. And it still is for the "better" students and, on the whole, has the better teachers.

The scientific division tends to separate science too much and too early from the totality of culture. Thus it may produce the technical expert who populates our universities and laboratories and fabricates more and more machines, but is unable to increase, perhaps even to understand, the knowledge of the basic theories which underlie the development of modern science.

Our commercial departments are in fact vocational schools for clerical work in business. They provide no training for those higher and complicated forms of organization and management which we find in important political and industrial positions. The organizer or executive of high rank is always a man of some understanding. He has a vision as to the conditions of the present and the possibilities of the future, much energy, and a feeling for the quality and reactions of people. This combination of faculties emerges out of a mixture of genuine talent, good education, and experience in areas related to the object of administration. But the wider the range of responsibilities in an administrative position, the less is it possible to provide its prospective bearer with a specialized training. What is the right secondary training for a Secretary of State, the director of a big company, the president of a great university, or the general of an army?

When the European nations had a surprisingly large number of successful men in all these fields, most of them had had a secondary education concentrating on Latin, Greek, mathematics, history, philosophy, and a limited number of great books, leaving the rest to later reading, personal interest, and to the experiences and tests of responsible adult life.

But these men may have become great because of fortunate external circumstance. Also, they lived in privileged families and a circle of friends in which they inhaled, as it were, the naïve egotism of a master group together with sensitiveness to human values — up to the point where the pursuit of these values did not encroach upon the prerogatives of class. This combination of class egotism with culture made it possible for them to combine with a good conscience imperialism with Christian faith, exploitation with charity, brutality with sensitiveness, and chauvinism with a feeling for international values.

The most promising of our youth do in fact prefer a broad liberal training to a narrow technical one. They generally do attend the "academic" divisions of our high schools. This trend of capable students imposes on us two tasks. The first is to reform these departments in such a way that they are not just narrow avenues for a mere theoretical training. They must aim at unity of knowledge, activity, and human understanding, for only so can they help the potential leader in politics and business. The other task must be to raise and widen the level of instruction in the commercial divisions so that they attract young people whose ambition and capacity go beyond the position of a clerk and typist.

We encounter another dilemma in respect to the fourth group we have set up, the manually gifted youth. The best form of schooling which uses primarily the manipulative and sensuous talents of young people for an all-round education, rather than simply for skill, has not yet been discovered. Most teachers do not yet see to what degree the senses and work with the hands can be used as stimuli for the development of thinking, taste, thoroughness, and initiative. Consequently, the vocational divisions are not attractive to ambitious teachers and students. Furthermore, as a result of our social conditions they cater to economic groups which young people prefer to escape from if they can. This is, after all, the result of American democratic mobility from which society and school profit in many respects, but for which we have also to pay the price.

The problems arising from this situation, together with the problem of organizing the fifth department for the youth without special gifts, will be faced in the next section. For such an exposition we are now prepared after having found the basic principle of policy. To say it once more: *though recognizing that there is a common field of experience also in certain basic intellectual pursuits, we must attempt to solve the dilemma between unity and diversity by using as the common core of education the activities primarily fitted to cultivate the emotions or the affective life.* For by necessity it becomes difficult and even impossible to enforce conformity the higher up we climb toward advanced intellectual activity. But rather than deploring or neglecting the great diversity of talent we should try to use it productively and in a spirit of gratefulness for the riches with which nature has endowed mankind.

B. THE IDEAL STRUCTURE

As viewed by other countries, the majority of the people of the United States are spoiled by external things: space, food, bathrooms, heating systems, buildings, movies, sports arenas, and perhaps even expectations for the future. It is difficult to understand, therefore, why our people are so satisfied with present public school buildings. Even the relatively new and big American schools are generally deficient from the architectural point of view. Most of them look as if they had been ordered from a department store. They could be much more inviting with respect to air and light, and from the viewpoint of some vision of what a school could really be they are unsatisfactory.

Why do Americans take it for granted that only the expensive independent colleges, the state universities, and private secondary schools may have a campus and a variety of buildings for various purposes, whereas the majority of our public schools consist only of one big building with depressingly long aisles which are dark, dreary, and in which hovers the typical smell of dusty classrooms?

Is it too presumptuous to expect that a secondary school in a sufficiently populated town could also have a large campus with several buildings, not just to imitate the vulgar idea of bigness, but to provide adequately and attractively for the variegated activities of the pupils?

Let us describe here the educational activities for which each of these buildings would be destined. In this description we shall be applying and testing the ideas developed in the first part of the chapter.

1. *Emotional Education*

If the visitor looks at the campus of our new school he discovers as the largest of all buildings the one in which all members of the school community assemble for their common activities. We call it, therefore, the Community House. Since the uniting element of our new education lies in the emotional sphere, this building would be the sanctuary for the cultivation of all those experiences and attitudes which enable both teachers and pupils to realize not only their oneness with their fellow men and all humanity, but also the relationship between man and the cosmos. Thus they should have in the Community House the inspirations of religion, beauty, and truth, not as possessions that make men proud, but as obligations, visions, and privileges.

But, can we have common religious elevation in our world of spiritual disunity and disintegration?

Our present civilization is uncreative in this respect. Most of our modern symbols are nationalistic; in consequence they divide mankind into hostile tribes instead of reminding it of unity. The most recent symbol, powerful and diabolic, was the swastika, which Hitler borrowed from medieval ornaments and ancient Asia. But it may well be that a generation whose emotional life is properly nourished together with its reason, may again become capable of expressing the deepest experiences of man: birth, love, death, light and darkness, in myths and symbols which elevate man rather than degrade him.

With this in mind there will be built into the Community House a chapel which, through the sacredness of its proportions, gives the visitor the feeling of embracing quiet and devotion. One of the values neglected in American education is spiritual rest and contemplation; so let the chapel be the place where a young person can go in order to be alone. In doing so he will also feel the profound comfort that can unite man with humanity and the universe, but only to the degree to which he dares go into and find his own self. There will be great poetry recited in the chapel and great music will be heard with the participation of the school choir and the school orchestra. Thus both the blessing which is in solitude and the blessing which is in belonging will be experienced.

If there are certain denominations which want their children to be imbued with their specific religious tradition, give them the opportunity, but outside the school. Our chapel will still prepare in young people the sense of reverence without which all human life degenerates into brutality. If certain groups refuse this participation then one may suspect that for them institution and sect are more important than religion, for which they claim to stand. Should they fear that the minds of the young may be contaminated by contact with a community that believes in the universality of religious experience despite all its various expressions, let them have their separate schools. Also, let those have their separate schools who do not want to have any transcendent idea in the education of their children, because hatred of religion becomes itself a sectarianism. The future will prove which attracts thinking parents more and turns out the better men: sectarianism in isolation or a great embracing faith.

Besides the chapel, the Community House harbors the art gallery, the music hall, the dramatic hall, and the general library. The purpose of each needs no long explanation. In the art gallery the student finds not only reproductions of the best paintings and etchings, but also originals loaned from the museums of town and state. Artists may like to exhibit their works. In the music hall the rehearsals and the performances of those concerts take place which are not fitted for the chapel; there is also a collection of records through which the student can acquaint himself with the great masterpieces of music, and individual booths for undisturbed and repeated listening. In winter the music hall may also serve as the domicile for the teacher of eurythmics and his pupils. For knowing of the close connection between education of the mind and education of the body, and knowing what the art of expressive gesture meant in the life of great peoples, we want to encourage in our youth this means of harmonious self-development.

The teacher of eurythmics will co-operate with the teacher in drama. In many of the great cultures the two arts belonged together; they both were a part of "music" in the great time of the Greeks because art then still grew out of the life of a creative community. Why should not our new school develop a style of festivals in which the whole community participates, and not only a few performers with a host of passive lookers-on? Certainly, the teacher of drama would justify his existence if he did nothing more than help the classes in English or other literatures transform printed words into words spoken and acted; but if he succeeded in motivating the pupils of a school to create their own drama, their own festivals, and perhaps their own symbols, he would do a still greater service to education.

Near the Community House the visitor of the new school would see the gymnasium and the surrounding play fields, which have an important part in the basic emotional education of the young. It may be that rhythmical education, rather than being connected with the Community House, should be connected with the sports center; there should be no dogmatic opinions about organizational problems. In any case, physical education should not be used primarily as an exercise of the muscles for the purpose of fighting down somebody else or as the occasional meeting ground for teachers and students — all shouting for the old school tie. There are apparently many schools and colleges which do not know any other way of uniting the community than by a football game. Nor should physical education be considered primarily a means of "character building" in the narrow sense.

Rightly understood, physical discipline is a part of education toward harmony and self-respect. It provides harmony in that a healthy and rhythmical, much better than a neglected body, can help a person in his desire for poise and balance; and it provides self-respect in that ethical values should not be the doubtful result of oversublimation and overcompensation, but organically interwoven with our physical existence. Only a false application of Christianity, with its thousandfold radiations into the philosophy and practice of life, could cause man to divorce the "physical" and "spiritual" sides of human nature. Thus our civilization has produced two dangerous representatives of one-sidedness: on the one hand the radical dualist who does not care for his body because he considers it the prison of the soul and the abode of sin, and on the other hand the sort of materialist for whom any mention of the spiritual side of man is anathema. The consequence is that in our Western civilization we have more broken existences and nervous breakdowns than even the inane hustle and bustle of our cities would seem to require. The whole confusion is reflected in certain Western concepts of sexual life with all the consequent conflicts and neuroses.

A clearer understanding of the laws of psycho-physical hygiene should lift the human being to a level where the tension between our urges and our morals could be reconciled by a new regard for the relation between human society and nature. Certainly there is no reason for shallow optimism — we cannot take conflict out of the universe by gymnastics and hiking clubs. But civilization would be advanced if education succeeded in awakening in our youth the sense of the strength, the beauty, and the law which are in all creation.

This, in brief outline, would be the new ethic of sport:

Respect your body because it is the instrument of mind and action, happiness and energy, effort and maturity.

Learn to use this instrument, and provide for it the conditions under which it can work most effectively. Do not pamper and do not abuse it; find the right balance between exercise and rest, exposure and protection, discipline and enjoyment.

Know that responsibility to your body is an obligation which you have not only to yourself, but to your fellow men, because they are happier with a sound and courageous person than with a physical or nervous wreck. Since the health of your body determines the health of your children, feel that you must be a strong link in the eternal chain of regeneration. And knowing how much you depend on your body, and how much your body depends on its environment, its food, and on the happiness of the soul, feel yourself responsible not only for yourself and your children but also for other people's happiness and welfare.

When you see a sick and crippled person, imagine how much he misses, help him, and pray that not through sickness, but through health you realize the blessing which lies in strength and vigor.

And when you swim in the ocean, and the sunny waves surround you; when you climb a mountain and God's landscape opens itself wider and wider to your enchanted eyes; when you see the trained body of an athlete swinging through the air as if he had overcome the law of heaviness: then inhale deeply all the beauty which nature can spend; imagine how generations of great artists have drawn inspiration from similar experiences; prove your gratefulness to the creator through fighting all that is destructive; and foster all that leads toward growth and productivity.

With sport understood in this way, there is no break between the "spiritual" and the "physical" in education. Then the whole group of activities, from the Community House with its chapel to the gymnasium and its play fields, would provide the area of basic emotional education in which all unite irrespective of their scholastic differences. There all should find safe foundation and constant help for the development of character and personality. Home rooms, assemblies, compulsory physical training, and other such plans in our better schools have long aimed at this goal. But if the student is not made conscious of the purposes, these activities become mere stereotypes; and if the teacher fails to understand their place in the totality of education he lacks the sense of proportion and overemphasizes sometimes the emotional and sometimes the intellectual sides.

2. Intellectual Education

Around the Community House we have the halls or houses for the various groups of pupils, divided according to their specific interests.

(a) *The Humanists.* There is the hall for the budding humanists. We do not prescribe a stiff pattern of curriculum. People who are unhappy without outlines, prescriptions, textbooks and other machinery should not become teachers. Hence, the program may vary according to the locality; some students may prefer the ancient, others the modern languages; some may be the prospective historians. But however many the ways, the goal is one. The boys and girls schooled in this division should be the future interpreters of the great humanist tradition on which our civilization rests. We do not ascribe to them the doubtful role of a perpetual guard of honor at the grave of the past. "Tradition," from the Latin *traditio*, means "handing down." It denotes the function of keeping constantly fresh the great reservoir of wisdom that the past may contain for the present and the future. The best wisdom dies unless it is continuously re-examined and renewed; it must serve as the challenge to do as well or even better than the dead who were not afraid of professing a revolutionary truth which their contemporaries disliked to hear.

At the school of the humanists we will not make things easy, nor will we rush through dozens of books, explained more or less amateurishly. We will rather go through the labor of learning some of the original languages in order to come closer to the mind of an author and his people. Especially, we will learn that interpretation of great documents is not just translating, but an imaginative art.

This art requires time for concentration and contemplation, so that we not only learn to read the letters, but grasp the spirit. Interpretation is not just linguistics, but *philology* in the profoundest sense, or "love of meaning"; it is not only reconstruction of words, but also re-formation of ideas, or transposition of things past into living attitudes and deeds. Identification with a great author is not acceptance of all his beliefs, but revival of the spirit behind and within him.

Only when we try to reason and act as the great men would exhort us to do if they could now talk with us, can they become our companions. All else is rightly accused of being an escape into the remote, and a futile exercise of the mind.

With this kind of spiritual guidance in the humanities all the other subjects will group themselves around it easily and organically. History will not be a lifeless enumeration of data, but an intercourse with the great thinkers and doers of earlier ages; it will be derived from the original documents and not be narrated in the customary textbook fashion. Mathematics and the sciences will be taught not so much with the intention of making mathematicians and scientists, but with the purpose of rounding out our knowledge and of giving us a sufficient insight into the character of exact disciplines and experimental research. Ignorance of the various methodical approaches of man to the great laws of life can be as dangerous as ignorance about humanity. Indeed, the two ignorances, as well as the two knowledges, always march together.

(b) *The Scientists*. With the same regard for a well-rounded aspect of the world, the students who concentrate on mathematics and science will not receive a merely "pre-professional" training.

The fundamental wisdom about man's relation to himself, his fellow men, and God has been expressed in the millennium before and during the end of antiquity, but unfortunately, the almost two thousand years which followed have not taught us much about the practical application of this wisdom to the problems of society. In this respect we are just as helpless as the ancient Greeks and Romans, a situation which, as everybody now knows, is all the more catastrophic as man's enormously increased mastery over nature has given him overwhelming powers. Consequently we must revert from the attitude of scientific isolationism as it emerged during the nineteenth century and reincorporate the exact and applied disciplines into a broader cultural and philosophical framework.

About the difficulty of this process we ought to have no illusions. But unless the school lays the groundwork there can be no hope. Thus, in the hall of the young scientists we will not try to drive the study of mathematics and the sciences so far that no time remains for a broad human development. In addition, we will not expose our students to the experience of graduates from certain secondary schools who are proud of their advanced scientific training until at college they discover that their high school teachers were not quite up to recent scholarship, so that they have first to unlearn and then to start all over again.

Needless to say, we will select teachers who are also scholars, but rather than insisting that they be topnotch scientists and technicians — who, anyhow, could not be attracted to secondary schools — we will choose the men and women for whom quantitative symbols and experiments are but another language invented by humanity in its endless search for the deeper meanings of the universe. Those who divide the landscape of the mind into a realm of the Spirit, with Plato in the center and the professors of the liberal arts genuflecting before his statue, and an area of inhuman scientific "exactness," are the most uncreative and illiberal educators, whether they are humanists or scientists. In *all* areas of knowledge there has to be the desire for reliable and honest methods, though methods applicable in one field may be unfitted for another. But there must also be inspiration. Exactness without inspiration creates mental agoraphobia.

(c) *The Executive Group.* The same combination of theory and application is requisite also for the education of our third group of students, the executive division. One could call their building "Franklin Hall" in order to place before their mind the image of one of the greatest servants of society, who combined practicality with high ideals, political skill with responsibility, and fellow-feeling for the common man with a strong sense for excellence. By his own initiative Franklin learned several languages. Though he fought for a new school which should be more useful than the obsolete classical training of his time, his outlook toward life was humanistic and liberal in the best sense.

The more we realize the difference between a Benjamin Franklin and the average young businessman, the greater must become our sense of responsibility. To be sure, there exists an excellent type of commercial employees who save a cultural life for themselves and their families in spite of all routine and competition. But one can also shudder at the emptiness that threatens the leisure time of so many young executives, clerks, salesmen, and technical employees for whom there is perhaps some sport and fishing, otherwise boredom or rather cheap amusement. Must these men and women really be as they are, or could twelve full years of school life not be used for better effect?

Why do we blame the cinema, the radio and television, the tabloids, and the advertisements? As long as businessmen selling this kind of merchandise work under competitive conditions they will fabricate what they hope to sell. And if industry and advertising were controlled by the government and competition restricted, we might run into other and even greater evils. Should we not blame the consumer who has so little pride and self-respect that he gleefully accepts inferior ware, and the schools who have failed to teach him what to accept and what to refuse, materially as well as spiritually?

Hence, even if we admit that the business section of the new secondary school may not be the school for training the higher executives and may, in general, have to do with more modest intellectual quality — even then we have to hold before the students an image of human excellence which inspires them to do their best. For any school cheats its pupils which fails to see that education is not merely a process of adjustment to the quality of the average, but a continuous motion between the two poles of ease and effort. If the teacher sets the goal too far away from the student's natural capacity, he may discourage him to the degree of final frustration. On the other hand, if education nicely adjusts itself to the student's and perhaps also to the teacher's desire for comfort, it fails to stimulate; and this is also a danger for education and civilization. To repeat, progressive education, truly understood, is not the elimination of all hardship in education, but the provision of joyful courage and self-discipline even in the hardships of learning. For what, so we may ask, is a teacher paid if he does not dare lead his pupils above the level of intelligence which they can just as well attain without him?

In Franklin Hall, therefore, we will explain not only the means and techniques of organization, business and management, but also the human goals which they have to serve. We will help them to understand the tradition on which our government and society are built, their differences from other political and social organizations, and the rights and duties of citizenship. They will learn one foreign language. And we will have the prospective businessmen as often as possible in the Community House, for perhaps even more than the young humanists they need a firm emotional basis for adhering to good standards of taste in a world of utility and competition.

Also, instead of spending too much time with the teaching of typewriting and other techniques which can be learned in special courses after or outside of high school, we will give the boys and girls from Franklin Hall a sense of good manual workmanship and send them frequently over to the fourth division of our ideal school where they will meet the young artisans.

(d) *The Artisans.* The building of this group will be one of the largest of the school community, because in addition to its classrooms it will contain a number of well-equipped workshops. These workshops, however, will not only be filled with the noise of tools and machines; they will in their own manner provide a wide, humanistically minded education. The difference will be in approach and kind, not in spirit and quality. We have already alluded to the pitiful fact that in our present school system the technical or "vocational" department is often the most neglected. In the manual division of our new school young people will be shown that technical work can also be a continual source of qualitative effort.

Since the Middle Ages teachers have realized the value of the crafts; the great Swiss educator Pestalozzi demanded the education of the hand just as much as that of the heart and the head. Up to the present the oldest and leading families of Europe taught their sons a craft. Only the hopeless intellectualism of modern so-called humanist and liberal schools could make people forget that the all-round education of a man does not come from the brain alone. Craft of high quality demands planning and thinking in relation to a concrete object; it demands devotion and accuracy, and, fortunately, it carries the test of efficiency immediately within itself. A philosopher of rank and unusual life experience once said to me: "The trouble with political and philosophical ideas is that they are not like cupboards. A badly made cupboard shakes and squeaks, but teaching the people false ideas can remain unnoticed until a whole society goes to pieces."

Without talking much about "art appreciation" and other abstractions, we will make the student conscious of the beauty inherent in a fine piece of craftsmanship, for each such piece reveals the unity of purpose, form, and material. We will not emphasize so much the modern fad of "originality" à tout prix, which often is nothing but another word for vanity and snobbishness. Rather our students will learn that true originality in art and craft comes only when the builder knows intimately the specific quality of his material and forgets himself over his work. If this sense for genuineness is once experienced, there may even be a transfer to more general problems of life. More or less by habituation the student may then develop a sort of trained instinct which helps him to distinguish quality from trash, truth from spuriousness, vagueness from clarity, and sentimentality from true idealism.

But there can be no transfer from one field into another unless a person possesses a certain spread of knowledge which makes association and comparison possible. The best-educated man will admit that he is often at sea when faced, say, with a political problem the premises and consequences of which he does not know. If the shadow of ignorance looms large among the educated, how much greater must its danger be among those who have neither much time nor interest in verbal information? Therefore the teachers in the artists' and artisans' department must seize every opportunity to point at the general problem inherent in a particular practical task. Sensuously gifted youth generally shy away from thinking in the thin atmosphere of abstraction. But a mathematical puzzle coming up in connection with a piece of carpentry, an architectural plan, or the building of an airplane may be attacked with courage and success. The same is the case with history and social relations. Discussed in logical isolation they are objects of horror to many a budding artisan and artist, but when connected with a practical issue they become relevant and interesting.

Hence we will use manual work not only as a value in its own right, but also as a center from which to move freely, yet systematically, into the sciences of both man and nature, especially in so far as they help the student to understand the interrelationship between his work and the culture of mankind.

(e) *The Workers.* But now the following question will arise: If all the four groups, the humanists, the scientists, the young executives, and the young artisans, are moving on a relatively high plane of achievement, who is going to take care of the many young people who are unable to live up to the high standards and who later will have to do the mechanical work in our plants and the routine activities on the farms?

There is something insoluble in the problem of educating the unskilled worker, because there is something insoluble in his human situation. To what degree can a feeling of value and meaningful participation be saved in our methods of mass production? To what degree can a man engaged in mechanized work go home, change his clothes, and be a completely different being? Is there perhaps a good deal of sentimentality in our belief in verbal forms of adult education? Would not a piece of garden land be much more useful? But where and how to secure it in our congested industrial areas? And will the worker and his wife be willing and able to do something with it? How protect them against unemployment, not only physically by relief measures, but in terms of adaptability and spiritual resources? What can the churches, the trade unions, the employers and the political communities do for the incorporation of the unskilled industrial and agricultural worker into the national culture?

These are problems in front of which all curriculum planning of teachers carries the stamp of snobbishness and imperfection. Our answer may point toward some constructive possibilities.

For the pupils without any particular ability we will provide a special, or fifth division, with a special house as its center. There they will be much happier and much more productive than in the so-called vocational sections of the typical modern city school. Just as much as the other boys and girls they will participate in the emotional education going on in the Community House. They will be instructed in the fundamentals of citizenship and husbandry. They will not suffer from the feeling that the knowledge extended to them is theoretical knowledge thinned and delivered in homeopathic doses; theirs will be strong and useful food, though simple. They will have their own workshops for semi-skilled work; they will help the students of the manual division to construct the apparatuses and tools necessary in the laboratories and classes of the school; they will assist the expert workers in the repair and upkeep of the buildings; they will work on the school farm, take care of its animals and plough its fields. For weeks and perhaps for months they may leave the school completely and work under the supervision and advice of teachers and experts on the great national task of reforestation and other forms of conservation of national resources. The geographical area of their activities may not even be restricted to this country. They may go to other parts of the world. Would they learn less by this manner of schooling? Certainly not. They would learn more, even theoretically, for they would discover the kinship between true learning and good acting, and there is probably no more valuable discovery than this.

The girls who are interested in household arts will act as the housemothers of the community. The whole division will be responsible for the roads, lawns, and flowers of the campus, and they will be the commanders of the squad when the young highbrows of the humanist and scientific groups come to work with them.

For there will be one rule in our school of the future: that every physically capable pupil will have to spend some hours of every week in useful practical work, partly in the workshops, partly on the farm and in the gardens. In the great effort to unite the individual members of the school into one community, and also to unite the various capacities in each individual into one harmonious whole, the Community House and the gymnasium on the one hand, and the workshops, the farm and the gardens on the other hand, will be equally important. They will be like the pillars holding the two ends of a bridge.

Only in a school with the spirit and equipment just described can we combine the two obligations in modern democratic education: respect for individual differences and respect for the community of men. The feeling of belonging, the training for sound character through proper cultivation of the emotions, learning, talking and practicing must be one united process. Democracy in education is not a reality if the students of the various divisions, while using the same entrance and exit of a big building, otherwise have nothing to do with each other. There must be a continual intercourse of young and lively people, but at the same time each of them must realize that he is in his proper place, and receive pride and incentive from this realization. Only in such a school — to go back to our critical remarks in Chapter II — can youth strive with a sense of happiness, only there can the conglomerate population of the United States be really united, and only there can man's nature and its inherent qualities be developed fully.

3. *The School in the Larger Community*

But all this is not enough. No institution, no movement, no idea, and no sentiment in the world can live long on itself — no family, no church, no country, no friendship, no love. A school community needs contact with the outer world in order to keep alive.

It is perhaps the greatest curse hanging over our schools that the teachers represent an isolated class with little participation in the social and political life of the community. The teacher has become more and more subject to suspicious control by petty community school boards and by misguided and misguiding politicians who mistake the country's safety with the arousing of hysterical timidity. How, under such circumstances, can a teacher stand before his class as a symbol of responsible maturity?

It will therefore be the attempt of our new school to become the center of cultural activities for the whole local community. The exhibits, concerts, and addresses given in the school will be frequented by the parents and the other inhabitants of the town; there they will receive advice about the education of their children, from the problems of diet and health up to the problems of mental and moral hygiene; and the teachers in the workshops, the gardens, and the farm will serve as the community consultants in all problems of husbandry.

At the same time — if possible in combination with the junior or the community college — the school will be the center for adult education, of a type which is more than vocational and more than a nice and harmless pastime. It will rather be education that helps the adult to clarify his own personal, social, and political problems in stimulating contact with other adults.

But where can we locate the new school and get the money for it?

Of course, it will have to be located at the outskirts of the city or town, for it will cover a large area. Some decades hence every modern city should be surrounded by a belt of green land beyond which, if the population increases, new suburbs may grow. On this belt will stretch the elementary and high schools; one, two, or ten, according to the size of the city.

Besides better educational and hygienic conditions, such an area belonging to our youth can have other important advantages. The social stratifications and cleavages in our society are reflected in the various regions of a city and, consequently, also in our schools. Just as there are well-to-do and poor city districts, so there are well-to-do and poor schools. In our present situation this is inevitable, though it is certainly not democratic. But if the schools were taken out of the narrow streets into one special and independent area to which children of the most varied parts of the city would flock, education would no longer have to fight the dividing effects of social grouping on the school system of the country. Furthermore, the parents as a whole, not just some portions of them, would be interested in one and the same school.

The big cities, which need dozens of such schools, will — let us hope — be decentralized in the meantime; for modern man will either become a sick man, or use his mastery of nature for sounder forms of living. Nor will transportation be a difficulty. Subways and parkways will lead toward the outskirts where the schools lie, and the children will not need more time for their way to school than they need now.

But who will pay for this whole expensive enterprise? Yes, expensive it will be! But it will be less expensive than the cigarettes the nation smokes, the liquor it drinks, and the social revolutions which are bound to come sooner or later unless our educational system is adjusted to the clearly recognized needs of modern society.

A further practical question remains. How can such a school be built in small towns and villages? Partly it can be done through co-operation of various communities. We already have consolidated high schools to which pupils come from wide distances. Should such pooling of forces be impossible, and the school have to remain small, even then one thing is possible: change the school from a center of verbalism into a center of culture; keep the young together where they like it, namely in a thoroughly planned physical and emotional education; and treat them individually where they have the right to be treated that way, namely in their more advanced intellectual activities. Often such a policy has arisen naturally out of the very smallness of a village school directed by one or two good teachers who enjoyed the help of the village parson for the instruction of the youth above the average. This is the reason why colleges are sometimes surprised that students with a rather "backward" education do so well in college; they do so because they were brought up under natural conditions, and they have enough accumulated energy which can be released on the higher level.

Those who began their university studies before World War I dreamt of a twentieth century different from what we have experienced so far. The century, expected to be one of enlightenment and progress, has turned out to be one of destruction and cruelty.

But why should not *one* of the great hopes which liberal men cherished at the start of this century become reality? We might create a school in which man's nature and man's nurture might become less and less divorced from each other, so that the coming generations might look at the world with a fresh mind willing and able to build a social order in harmony with the inner conditions of human development.

Fortunately, there already are a number of schools in the United States whose leaders and teachers have understood this responsibility. Much of what has been assumed in this chapter on the school of the future is for them no longer utopia, but part of an emergent reality. But the new schools and their teachers need support. And this support can become strong and persuasive only if there works behind and within it the necessary degree of clarity in regard to the principles which are guiding the action.

CHAPTER FOUR

Philosophy of Secondary Education

THERE IS A CLOSE RELATION between action and philosophy. Philosophy without action is empty; action without philosophy is blind. For if there is no philosophy behind and within an action, there is little hope for productive continuity. All continuity requires plan, method, and the endeavor to enclose the more immediate goals and purposes into ever-widening horizons of relevance and comprehension. If extended far enough these horizons blend into the metaphysical. For there is in us all a desire for something comprehensive. However dimly conceived, it appears to us both as a symbol of high quality and as a challenge to harmonize the relative and finite character of all human work with the more abiding values of existence. All that we dare call "perfect" has these attributes.

Therefore we demand that the makers of socially far-reaching plans present us not merely with an assembly of general ideas issuing into a haphazard process of trial and error, but prove their capacity for integrating their thought into a whole which is both philosophically and practically defensible.

Since in the preceding chapter we made detailed suggestions with respect to the curriculum of the various groups, it might now be profitable to recall first the over-all picture of our ideal school. For this purpose we could choose the symbol of five pyramids arising from a common foundation. The foundation represents the common physical, emotional, and character-building education of all students. The Community House, the workshops, the campus, and the farm would offer the locations for these common and socializing activities.

The pyramids, on the other hand, symbolize the differentiated formal learning of the five groups: the humanists, scientists, executives, artisans, and workers. Each pyramid, though having its base in common with all others, is inclined in a different direction — direction indicating the special education given to each of the five groups. Some of the pyramids differ also with respect to altitude, supposing that altitude represents the degree and extent of scholarly performance demanded from each group. From the young humanists and scientists, for example, a higher power of abstraction is required than from the young artisans and workers.

Since all the pyramids with their varying inclinations have the same base, they necessarily intersect in a large part of their volumes. This means that, the differences of specialization notwithstanding, a large part of the same subject matter will be taught in the study programs of the five groups, so that in the lower grades a student can transfer from one group to another without too much loss of time. This possibility of transfer is important because only in this way can immobility, injustice, and early frustration be avoided.

In other words, in addition to the physical-emotional-character-building training common to all, there will also be common layers of subject matter and intellectual experience. The farther one goes up the pyramids, the smaller becomes the range of communality, as is the case with all specialization, both in our modern schools and in our whole modern civilization. The farther one goes down the pyramids, the more they have in common with the others. Specialization in science must rest, for example, on the knowledge of certain basic areas of learning which are shared by all students, down to the common core of public education provided by our elementary schools. But, to repeat, even during the years of more intensive specialization and separation of subject matter the pupils of our new school will live in strong communality because of their participation in the foundational cultivation of body and soul.

So far, however, we have dealt mainly with problems of inner organization, based on an understanding of the psychological conditions of learning in a democratic situation with its demand for a combination of quality and equality.

We now pass to a more systematic treatment of the values and attitudes we hope to achieve in our new school.

Many books have been written and many battles fought about the underlying goals of secondary education. In our present American civilization the prospective teachers hear especially about the seven cardinal principles already referred to at the beginning of Chapter III. They emphasize the values of health, command of fundamental processes, worthy home membership, vocation, citizenship, worthy use of leisure, and ethical character. Charles A. Beard's ideas about the responsibilities of the American public school have also been mentioned. The Harvard Committee Report on *General Education in a Free Society* speaks in general terms about "the good life." All such definitions, of course, depend upon the particular culture from which they spring. The Puritans, as well as modern Catholic or Protestant educators, would miss in them emphasis on the "supernatural" forces in which, according to their opinion, all human endeavor should be embedded, while authoritarians and totalitarians would consider them too individualistic. The attempt at defining educational aims runs into the same difficulties as the attempt at setting up a catalogue of moral aims in general. There will be agreement about many individual virtues, but even their interpretation will be colored by one's opinions with respect to the place of man and his society in the universe, and about the universe itself.

Thus, instead of discussing the final goals toward which education has to strive, let us concentrate on some functional value attitudes which our ideal school community should achieve as it operates.

Rather than writing another general treatise on education and ethics, we shall speak of the necessity of both conformity and non-conformity as determinants in the life of a mature citizen. After that we will describe certain appreciations which the secondary school should convey to its students. First, an appreciation of the ego-transcending quality of a worthy life; second, an appreciation of the values of persistence and of the seeing of relationships; third, a sense for the kinship between the theoretical and the practical life; fourth, the courage of self-assurance; and fifth, the desire for a liberal or general education. After this, some final and more technical questions will be discussed.

A. Values and Attitudes

Adolescence, like childhood and adulthood, has its own value and character; it is not merely a transition period. However, it represents the period when, often with inner conflicts, man grows from childhood to adulthood, from immaturity to the expectation of maturity.

1. *The Values of Conformity and Non-Conformity and the Consciousness of the Transcendent*

(a) *Balance and Conformity.* Who is mature? There are physical characteristics about maturity which in our school we will respect by encouraging the various activities of sport, eurythmics, and physical hygiene. In this context, however, we will deal with mental maturity, realizing fully that it defies any satisfactory definition. Maturity can be described only in terms of behavior. We call a person mature who knows how to master somewhat successfully the tasks which his society can properly expect him to meet. Though not without occasional disturbances, such a person will achieve a certain balance between the demands he accepts as justified from his group, the goals he sets up for himself, and the capacities he possesses. If the tasks and goals are beyond his capacity, the result will be intimidation; if they fall behind, the result will be frustration. A person is mature who — as far as is humanly possible — understands himself and his environment in a continuing process of growth.

This, of course, is an ideal state which no individual fully achieves. Few people have the good luck to find the society which fits exactly their capacities and desires and, at the same time, has a constantly stimulating influence. Others do not possess the external means necessary for their full development; the work which many people are compelled to do is routine and mechanical, and consequently stifling rather than encouraging. Furthermore, our society by necessity is based on conventions, and while there are many people for whom these conventions are difficult, there are others, the creative and richly endowed, for whom they are like chains around a growing limb. Into this category belong those who rebel out of superiority and abundance: the social reformers, the discoverers of new truths, the adventurers, the great lovers, and the creative artists through whom life speaks more loudly and vigorously than convention tolerates.

In addition there are differences in temperament. For some people, life is like a merry-go-round; for others it is a continuous struggle. And there are differences in social adjustment. Not even in the most ideal democracy could there be achieved a complete balance between the individual and the whole. Such balance is not even desirable. All one may hope is that normally in a good society the group and the individual will support each other, and that the inevitable tensions will be of a productive nature. But we should not forget that certain aristocratic cultures, e.g., the Renaissance, have seemingly shown a greater appreciation for the exceptional individual than cultures based on typical middle-class agreement.

Really mature people and societies will strive for balance but, at the same time, recognize the value of unbalance, provided it comes from superiority. If a serious individual feels in himself the moral right of protest and exception, he may act accordingly, provided he knows that he exposes himself to a fight the scars of which he may always carry with him.

As things are in a lively society, so they ought also to be in a lively education. Schools cannot attempt to breed rebellious geniuses, though progress depends on them. They must aim at educating people who live with, rather than against, their society. But this ought not to be mistaken for education toward conventionalism and conformity. "Adjustment" is only a partial goal in the process of education toward maturity. A person who wishes nothing more than to be adjusted is a coward. "Before man made us citizens, great Nature made us men" (James Russell Lowell).

(b) *The Value of Non-Conformity.* But here the question arises: Where is the source of justifiable non-conformity? Or, to phrase it more contradictorily, where is the legitimate source of that kind of illegality without which there is no progress in man and his society? The source lies in something which is highly subjective. Consequently, it is exposed to profound error, as is anything apprehended mainly by faith and personal intuition. But at the same time it is objective, or at least super-personal, in that it must be greater than mere individual interest. When a man dares to set non-conformity against conformity, liberty against law, he always should feel a loyalty to values greater than his ego, greater than society, and greater than written law. His values must not be egocentric, they may not even be sociocentric; rather they must be cosmocentric. In spite of all passionate interest in a specific idea or action, he must be convinced of its harmony with trends and laws which, when once understood by his fellow men, will lift them above routine and convention into spheres of greater truth and freedom. In men such as Socrates and Giordano Bruno there was a feeling of unity with the order of the universe which gave them the right to offend the conventions of men.

(c) *The Consciousness of the Transcendent.* Only such a school makes adolescents mature which, together with giving them a sense and capacity for adjustment to society, i.e., a sense for conformity, gives them also a sense for the value of non-conformity. This means a sense for values which have inspired men to put the demands of their conscience above personal interests and social pressures. Only a school which does not simply teach youth to respect sound human conventions and laws, but also shows the relativity of human institutions before the deeper dimensions of value, is democratic. For all democracy depends upon the acknowledgment of the superiority of the *ratio universalis* over the *ratio particularis*. When this ever-transcendent consciousness no longer exists, a society is gliding down the slope toward ruthless imperialism, exploitation of the weaker, and finally totalitarianism and despotism. Hence these seemingly abstract speculations are not "remote," but carry with them the weight of stern and unyielding reality.

All religions speak of this extension of the personality into the Infinite without which there is no peace or happiness. Only people who admire science without understanding its limitations fail to recognize that the extension of the personality beyond itself, or the transcendent character of all human life, is an indispensable requisite of civilization and not merely a subject for theologians and metaphysicians. Psychiatrists find the source of nervous diseases, and the lack of resistance to disturbing experiences, in modern man's isolation, in his living without destiny, and in his individualist divorce from universality. By separating himself from the whole, man does not become an individual, but lonely and restless. Without the recognition of this fact, our civilization may produce more and more schools and pride itself on abolishing illiteracy, but it will produce less and less maturity; it will cry for more and more education, but will have more and more uncertainty.

But how can we break through this vicious circle?

Certainly not through offering our adolescent students theological exhortations or the sort of philosophical analysis which in this present context has been necessary for the understanding of our cultural situation. If the fundamental experiences, which have here to be explained in abstract language, could not actually be had by the farmer and worker just as much as by the scholar, they could not serve as the foundation of public education, for public education aims essentially at the totality of the normal people.

Here we point once more to the importance of emotional and practical education in our new school. The worship, the various arts, the higher form of community life cultivated there, are not just a way of passing the time, not even a form of beautiful esthetic elevation — though they ought to be that too. Rather they are the foundation on which all other education has to rest if it is to be meaningful. For only the rooted person can integrate his experiences and knowledge instead of just adding one impression to the other.

Fortunately, all developed nations possess masterpieces of folk literature, plastic arts, and music which immediately appeal to every normal heart and mind. From such art, through which the soul of mankind speaks with the grandeur of simplicity, one may lead the pupil gradually to the understanding of more difficult creations. It was Brahms who said that with all his talent he could not achieve the beauty of a certain old German folk tune which every child was able to sing.

Consequently, art education does not need to force upon students with unprepared minds the dramas of Shakespeare or the last sonatas of Beethoven. By beginning with the simple but unadulterated, however, and thence ascending to higher levels, both the pupils and the teachers might find out that the very greatest art and thought contain elements of depth accessible to everyone who is willing to understand. These remarks should not be interpreted to say that every simplification of a complicated work is objectionable. There is an immense difference between simplification and distortion.

Two methods of acquainting people with great works of art and thought, though seemingly contrasting, are equally dangerous, because both spring from disrespect for quality. One method is to begin by offering great and difficult works but to chase the authors out of them by all kinds of "rearrangements," so that every school boy believes he can pat Dante or Milton on the back. The other equally mistaken method is to begin with the vulgar because it "appeals," with the benevolent intention of gradually "lifting the masses up" to higher levels. The first practice is offensive to the creative genius, the other to the genius of the people whom the educator has to serve. For though, out of inertia, every people falls easily prey to cheap offerings, it actually wants and welcomes the better, as inexpensive good musical and theatrical performances have proved all over the world.

2. *The Value of Persistence and the Seeing of Relationships*

In addition to the sense for the ever-widening and transcendent horizons of excellence, there are other characteristics of maturity for which the high school has to prepare. These are persistence and the seeing of relationships. Training in persistence is necessary because only that person can develop his qualities to the best who does not relax when "things get tough." And upon persistence depends the seeing of relationships. A mind which does not persevere, contemplate, and use effort will discover contacts between various entities only when they border on each other, but it will not see the wider frame and the higher plane where they all unite.

Nor can there be maturity without the seeing of relationships. This capacity, if highly developed, was called by

Plato the art of dialectics and rightly considered as the medium through which man could arrive at a comprehensive philosophy of life. Certainly we cannot demand from an adolescent what today only a few adults are able to achieve; however, we should and can organize the high school program in such a fashion that it leads the pupil toward holistic rather than atomistic thinking.

It is interesting to read the *Report of the Committee of Ten on Secondary School Studies* of 1893 and the *Proceedings of the Committee on College Entrance Requirements* of 1899, both of which, together with the Retirement System of the Carnegie Foundation, are responsible for the general introduction of the unit system in the American high school.

In consequence of the rapid growth of the secondary school system in a decentralized setting, and in consequence also of the influx of new scientific subjects into the traditional program of studies, the two committees found themselves before a bewildering situation which was not easy to remedy. In the times of President Eliot of Harvard, who was the chairman of the Committee of Ten, himself a scientist, and living in the age when science was supposed to occupy the seat of the liberal arts, what was more likely than to try a merely formal and quantitative solution? Rather than consider the introduction of an adolescent into the culture of the adults as an organic and interconnected process, one divided the program of the high school into "course units," expecting that an applicant to a college should have assembled about sixteen such units. There are some remarks in the minutes of the Committees which testify that they still wanted "every youth who entered college" to "have spent four years in studying a few subjects thoroughly." But at the same time the Committee of Ten opened the way toward the defeat of this requisite by stating that it worked "on the theory that all the subjects are to be considered equivalent in educational rank for the purpose of admission to college." Therefore, it would make no difference which subjects a college applicant had chosen for his program: he would presumably have had four years of strong and effective mental training.

Of course, this optimistic assumption was expressed in an historical situation when the secondary school was still mainly a selective school for college aspirants and consequently much more uniform than at present. Furthermore, the Committee of Ten based its recommendations on the demand, expressed by the ninety-eight teachers who acted as advisors, "that every subject which is taught at all in a secondary school should be taught in the same way and to the same extent to every pupil so long as he pursues it, no matter what the probable destination of the pupil may be, or at what point his education is to cease. Thus for all pupils who study Latin, or history or algebra, for example, the allotment of time and the method of instruction in a given school should be the same year by year. Not that all the pupils should pursue every subject for the same number of years; but so long as they do pursue it, they should all be treated alike."[1]

For the purpose of determining this equal treatment the experts worked out a study plan for every subject. It is nevertheless hard to understand how the teachers and the Committee members could trust their own recommendations: opening the way for the greatest amount of freedom in the choice of electives in high school and college (which was an historical necessity), and believing at one and the same time that within that complete freedom, and within

[1] *Report of the Committee of Ten on Secondary School Studies,* published for the National Education Association by the American Book Company, New York, 1894.

the most decentralized school system of the Western nations, every subject could and would be taught "in the same way and to the same extent to every pupil."

President Baker of the University of Colorado wrote a minority opinion, but his warnings remained unheeded.

For the purpose of reckoning and for the purposes of the Carnegie Foundation which needed some statistical criteria to determine which colleges should enjoy the privileges of the retirement plan, the recommendations of the Committee of Ten proved to be useful. They were supported by the prestige of an atomistic psychology which cut the process of intellectual maturing into little pieces, had no regard for the complex conditions of culture as a whole, and was supposed to have proved "scientifically" that it did not make any difference when you learned, what you learned, and in what context.

The result of this credit system has been that today a pupil can go through high school with a miscellaneous program of studies. He may try a year of French, and if he does not like it, he may drop it. He may have some science and mathematics in the ninth grade, then forget about it in the tenth and eleventh grades and take it up again in his senior year. If these subjects are too difficult, he may change over to social science and typewriting. In short, he may have a little bit of everything without anything being based on or leading up toward something. Only English and American history are required. This system provides flexibility, but it is the flexibility of chaos. It is contrary to the ideas of the great theorists of education; it is contrary to the practice of any country which has had good schools. It is also contrary to common sense and common experience, for we all know that we cannot remember something we have quickly begun and quickly dropped, something we have learned without any relation to what we already know and what we intend to do in the future. Rather than creating order and knowledge, such learning creates confusion. Can we then wonder that intelligent young people come to our colleges and may rightly be asked by their instructors what in heaven's name they have done during twelve full years of previous schooling?

As a matter of fact, they may have been constantly busy, but like a mason who is laying bricks without any direction and system. As long as this practice can exercise its influence on the minds of the students and the faculty, all our theoretical knowledge about the laws of learning will be useless, all the other fine qualities of the American schools will not enable them to compete with the scholastic achievements of good schools in other nations, and educators who visit this country, though first impressed by all the various activities, will after a while become critical and ask toward what end all this teaching, guiding, and testing is supposed to lead.

The glory of the American school system has been its democratic character. Today other countries also, though in different ways, move toward the goal of educational justice. This, then, will no longer be the mark of distinction on which America can pride herself. But there is danger that our schools forget more than those of other countries that pieces of information do not create mental formation, and that freedom in education is productive only within an embracing order, but not if pupils constantly have to choose and do not know how and for what. Needless to say, ideal harmony between order and freedom can never be achieved. All human thinking proceeds in segments. And, somehow, we all have to specialize the moment we climb beyond the level of rudimentary and foundational learning. But the partialities which are in our mortal nature should not degenerate into closed patterns and into an assemblage of isolated entities. Each approach we try should aim toward a certain rounded-ness of view. Only thus can the parts complement each other and awaken in the student the sense for inter-relation-ships, or a consciousness of the fact that there are different ways but only one world.

The young humanists in our ideal school should, for ex-ample, be the kind of people who like to understand life primarily through the interpretation of the great thoughts and deeds of men. Human self-expression, its depth and its content, should play an eminent role in their education. The various languages should be taught in such fashion that the pupil understands the grammar and syntax of words as means toward the goal of ordering the fortuitous impres-sions of man in a manner that allows for clarity, depth, and communicability. But today our language teachers cannot even agree on the use of a uniform technical vocabulary for denoting the rules applying to the various languages taught in one and the same school. How, under such conditions, can there be effective transfer from one language to the other? Furthermore, interest in the nature and meaning of words should be provided through comparative interpre-tation of the vocabulary of the various Indo-Germanic languages. The readings should be so chosen that they present characteristic expressions in the growth of human culture and also appeal to the student's life and curiosity.

The way in which, for example, some teachers of Latin teach this language and select texts for reading, even in good and progressive schools, is certainly not inviting. The young neophytes in ancient culture must receive the impression that the Latin civilization created nothing but Caesar's *Bellum Gallicum* in which, naturally, an American student is not particularly interested. That St. Augustine who helped to lay the foundation of our Christian civilization also used Latin, that the Romans were the great lawgivers, that Latin was used by the great thinkers of Europe up to the seventeenth and eighteenth centuries — all this remains unnoticed by most American students of Latin.

When, finally, in some selected classes the student climbs up to the heights of Cicero and Horace, there often is neither philosophy, nor law, nor poetry in this teaching, but just translating. Then we wonder that boys and girls lose taste for the "classics" and "liberal education." They are not wrong; their teachers are.

The teaching of literature should be supplemented by the teaching of history But it should not happen again and again that students know better than their teachers how it should be taught. A few days ago I received the following letter from a student of one of the best high schools in the country:

Recently in a very interesting history class concerning the power of the Federal Government as opposed to the sovereignty of individual states we discussed nothing but facts, such as important events and decisions which had repercussions on this question. Nothing was mentioned about the importance of both standpoints and their theories. It is such a pity because so much is being missed. In studying for tests we fill our heads with facts; afterwards we never remember them and since we have not become acquainted with ideas we learn almost nothing.

In the curriculum of the humanists, mathematics and the sciences should be taught in such a manner that they are illustrations and explanations of human culture which, after all, is a continual revelation of order in a world of strife. Only thus can the student experience the essential unity in man's twofold approach to the mysteries of the universe: one approach carried out by dint of word concepts, the other by dint of number concepts. If educated in that way he will dislike the split in the thinking of so many college professors for whom the humanities represent the "liberal" and "philo-sophical," and the sciences the "exact" studies, each camp always looking down at the other.

The humanist student who is offered an interconnected curriculum will also understand the intimate relation be-tween the work of the mind and the work of the hand. For he will spend some time in the workshop where he will learn that civilization becomes possible not only through the ideas and deeds of outstanding individuals, but also through the common man's labor. And when he deals with the writings of great thinkers in the field of science he will personally test their truths or errors in the laboratory, the equipment of which has not been bought ready-made but built by the students themselves.

The great biological processes of life he will observe in the farm and the fields of the school.

The same demand for the wholeness of the curriculum applies also to the other divisions of the school, but with different emphases of interest and subject matter according to the specific goals of each group. For every graduate should carry with him one priceless possession, the greatest that a school can give. Since his learning will have been in harmony with his personal development, he will not only have found his own self, but will know how to develop it further through that continual process of expansion and integration which is the characteristic of healthy growth.

As Confucius says in a chapter on Central Harmony:

When our true central self and harmony are realized, the uni-verse then becomes a cosmos and all things attain their full growth and development.[2]

---

[2] *The Wisdom of Confucius*, edited and translated with notes by Lin Yutang, New York, The Modern Library, 1938, p. 104.

3. *The Kinship between Theory and Practice*

But all wise men have emphasized as requisites for inner maturity not only a vision of the transcendent, a persevering mind, and the seeing of relationships. They have also laid stress on the continual interchange between learning and action, or theory and responsibility, or the *vita contemplativa* and the *vita activa*. We have referred to this essential factor in all real learning, and described the various practical duties which the pupil of our new high school will have to fulfill. Only the man who knows both sides of life, the theoretical and the active, really knows what life is. He has learned that it is pluralistic and multidimensional, a mixture of rational and irrational factors, a continual surprise which can never be mastered by mere expertship, but, in the most fortunate case, by wisdom.

For this reason Plato insists in *The Republic* that the future philosopher-guardians of the State not be permitted to devote themselves exclusively to the study of dialectics. They should go "down into the cave again" (the cave being the symbol for the dark and irrational forces of life) and take over practical responsibilities so that they may not "fall short of the other type of experience either."

4. *Self-Assurance*

The fourth of the several elements of maturity to be mentioned is the mood of self-assurance which issues from the possession of knowledge sufficient to make a person at home in his civilization and capable of communicating with his fellow men. This knowledge cannot be the same for all, nor does it need to be. A farmer will always feel most at home among his fellow farmers, a workman among his fellow workmen, and a physician among physicians. There is no sense of inferiority in a man's realization that people from other vocations know more about their specific activities than he. It comes from a man's feeling of ignorance and inefficiency in matters where he is rightly expected to be informed.

But only the dull person is satisfied merely with his "job." In contrast to the dull, a person who may willingly admit his ignorance in foreign fields of knowledge or in comparison with superior minds, is rightly filled with resentment when he becomes aware that he could do so much better if his schooling had been adequate to his intelligence. Nobody likes to live below the level which his potential talent allows. The resentment that springs from frustrated development helps to explain the strange mixture of overadmiration and hostility which the self-conscious proletarian worker feels in his relation to the college graduate. "If I had had all his wonderful education, I would be a much better man than he." It also explains why Francis Bacon's words, "Knowledge is power," are so often cited in proletarian writings and speeches; they suggest to the workers the idea that knowledge means more self-certainty, more security, and more influence. Unfortunately, they fail to suggest at the same time that knowledge is also modesty and sacrifice. Sometimes it may even be the gateway toward inner conflict.

5. Liberal Education

Here we detect the human and philosophical meaning of liberal education in a democratic society. This education is not a collection of fragments of knowledge destined to provide the owner with a little information about everything and anything. Liberal education is not even the same as "general" education. The latter has a quantitative connotation and leads to encyclopaedic knowledge, whereas the first is a matter of inner enrichment and personal responsibilities. It must be conceived of as that body of basic experience and knowledge which helps an individual to feel himself both as an understanding and as an understood member of his group. He ought to feel this unity with his fellow men not only in the pursuit of immediate practical purposes, but also in regard to the essential human values inherent in the tradition and vital for the future. It is the cruelty of destiny, though at the same time its challenge, that for the richly endowed the share will be greater than for the less privileged. But this inevitable inequality is no excuse for the failure to provide for everybody as great an opportunity as possible to participate in the fundamental and common heritage of mankind.

Those who have understood the meaning and role of liberal education will necessarily be suspicious of early and narrow vocational training. For such a training often gives the students a kind of knowledge which could easily be learned in practice, but which separates them at the same time from sources of human enrichment. Man needs guidance most of all in those activities which are not immediately understandable and aim at purposes of wide and comprehensive range. Therefore young people, in their natural desire to see the fruits of their labor and to prove their usefulness to themselves and others, are slow to see the blessings of a liberal education. But if it is provided in a stimulating form many adolescents follow their teachers with ardent interest, for, feeling thrown out of the protective slumber of childhood and stirred up by all kinds of personal and social problems, they are anxious to find some order behind the threatening chaos. Hence, liberal education is philosophical in spirit — which is not at all the same as instruction in philosophy.

However, this defense of liberal education does not reject practical subjects. After all that has been said so far this should not need emphasis. We have to cultivate not only the head, but also the heart and the hand. There will be a difference in emphasis according to a person's belonging to a particular group of talents, but this difference must not preclude the communality in the basic activities and interests of the race.

Often the terms "liberal" and "general" are used synonymously, following a certain loose usage in modern educational literature.[3] But, as already indicated, there is a danger in this identification. Doubtless, it is difficult to have a free, or liberal, mind without some knowledge related to the common, or general, concerns of mankind. But the liberal as such is not in the knowledge but in the attitude, so that a man with much knowledge may not have a liberal mind, whereas a deep and sensitive person with less knowledge may have. The general tends easily toward the accumulative; the liberal tends toward the ethical. The general tends toward universality in terms of width, which today is an impossibility; the liberal tends toward universality in terms of inner communication. And this is the only universality which is possible.

B. THREE FINAL QUESTIONS

There arise now three final questions: the first, the age levels on which the ideal high school and the various degrees of differentiation should begin; the second, the selection of

---

[3] See, e.g., *General Education in a Free Society*, Report of the Harvard Committee, Harvard University Press, 1946.

the pupils according to their potential talents; and the third, the compatibility of our school with the democratic ideal of social justice.

1. *The Age Level*

The student should begin his career in the new high school after six years of elementary education. Needless to say, we would like to have boys and girls as early as ten and eleven years of age in a school environment which would allow for a better cultivation of their emotional life, for interesting impressions, and for more differentiation and elasticity in learning than the typical elementary school offers. It is an experience of parents in many countries that their children who like their school up to the age of nine or ten get bored, uninterested, and consequently rebellious thereafter.

However, if we want in our ideal school the system of co-operating houses, a high degree of self-administration and mutual contact among the various groups of students, and if, finally, the school is to serve as a kind of community center, then it should not accept pupils before the age of about twelve. Indeed, that is the time when many communities begin the junior high school.

This scheme, allowing for a certain degree of flexibility even in the early years of high school, resembles the older European pattern. Yet our system would differ from the European in that it keeps all children, whether they will be scholars or workers, within the same school community. It would provide for them a larger body of common experience than our big high schools where, as has been said, the pupils of the college preparatory and the vocational divisions have often not much more in common than the same entrance and exit.

The other essential difference between the older European

pattern and our new high school would be that in our scheme every promising pupil would be admitted to higher education from whatever division he may come, though the graduates from a more intellectual division have by necessity a greater chance to succeed in a liberal arts college than those from other divisions. This is inevitable; how many graduates from vocational high schools now attend our colleges and universities? But in our present public school systems the more practical training not only precludes almost all of its students from higher education, but it is also in itself less attractive and purposeful than it could be. In contrast, when a student leaves the more practical divisions of our new school he should be prepared for a later living with wife and children not less rich in the possibilities of depth and enjoyment than that of anybody else. The deepest values of man do not depend on sophistication. To be sure, against the injustices and vicissitudes of employment and unemployment even the best school has no remedy. All it can hope for is to educate a person so that he is able to meet the difficulties of life with a reservoir of courage, initiative, and inner solace.

But to return to our main topic. Which of the two systems is preferable, earlier or later beginning of differentiation? Those who believe they have the complete answer generally overlook the innumerable factors entering into the picture. As a matter of fact, the discussion about earlier or later separation of students is raging all over the civilized world. The advocates of later differentiation claim that they do so in the name of "democracy," for according to their scheme young people would be kept together for a long time. In addition the threat would be avoided that school separation means the fostering of social classes. But then one would have to explain why such countries as Switzerland, the Scandinavian nations, the Netherlands, and Britain have achieved a high democratic culture, perhaps a higher one than we have here, despite the strong and early articulation in their school systems. After all, whether a country turns toward democracy or not is decided by forces more powerful than the structure of its schools; it is decided not only by the weight of economic and political factors, but also by the moral and spiritual climate of the total society.

2. *Criteria for Selection*

As to the second problem, what are the criteria for selection? Naturally, the American teacher envisages "batteries of tests." One may dislike the term "battery" for its connotation of cruelty, for "battery" means literally the act of beating. But one should have nothing against careful testing. Education and our whole society can profit from the science of psychometrics, if it is wisely applied. If it is not, then the "batteries" drawn up before our youth may destroy the meaning and effect of education.

Testing as is customary in the United States is a process of examination, and examinations determine by necessity the process of instruction. If a teacher, say in French, has to give a "true and false" test every week, then his teaching and the learning of his students will resemble much more a hurdle race than a quiet, coherent and organic process of forming young personalities. Little room will be left for occasional excursions away from vocabulary and grammar into the culture and history of France and for discussion and exchange of ideas; the prevalent feature of the classroom activities will be drill.

American teachers, provided they know nothing about foreign school systems, generally take comfort for their low salaries in the assumption that the teachers in the adminis-

tratively centralized countries with their ministries of education are more restricted in their freedom of teaching. On
the contrary, in spite of all prescriptions and regulations
issued from the central educational authorities in the European countries, their instructors have better chances to
arrange their instruction freely within the scope of a year's
program than does an American test-haunted teacher. Don't
Americans see that their national test agencies exercise just
as great, if not a greater, dictatorial power over the teacher
as the European ministries of education, except in totalitarian situations? When Professor William Stern of Ham-
burg, who with the Frenchman Binet was one of the first
pioneers in testing, had been for two years in this country
as a political refugee, he told me that he was shocked to see
the final influence of Binet's and his own endeavors on
American education.

A teacher's judgment on a student may sometimes be
unreliable, but I am not yet convinced that tests fabricated
by agencies outside the school, by College Entrance Boards
and other bureaucratic authorities, can ever replace the
opinion of an experienced teacher. Our good colleges know
that and consequently use both.

Thus, through a mixture of personal interviews and tests,
pupils definitely fitted or unfitted for one or the other division of our school could be properly advised. And for the
large middle group, about whom it is difficult to speak with
finality, the first two years of more general instruction should
give sufficient ground for orientation.

But all this requires an organic continuity of instruction.
And here we return again to the demand already raised:
change the formalistic and mechanical concept of an educational program and curriculum in favor of an organic concept

of mental growth and education. Do so for the sake of our youth and for the sake of the whole country!

3. The Postulate of Social Justice

Third, and finally, it may be good to forestall the reproach of advocating an "undemocratic" school system because of the recommendation that the pupils be classified according to their talent. There have always been divisions within the bigger high schools; also, there have been many highly selective private schools, especially in the older parts of the country. There have been parochial schools and enormous differences of educational chance and quality in the various states. Also money and the father's social position have always played a role. Let us hope we can increasingly avoid the latter evil by a sound scholarship system for the truly gifted children from financially less fortunate families. Some of the other "inequalities" will remain, however, simply because the Lord apparently liked plurality in his creation more than uniformity. If we abhor totalitarianism we do so, I hope, not only because we do not like the political competition of communist or fascist countries, but also because we consider their collectivism against human nature.

Speaking positively, a school system is sound only to the degree to which it helps young people toward a vigorous and constructive life. Such preparation is impossible without the risk of certain conflicts in the souls of pupils. If the prime goal of education were to spare their feelings at any price it would create as much frustration and disappointment as an educational system running on the principle: "The harder, the better." If a school, in consequence of false leniency or lack of discrimination, allows a student to overestimate his capacity, this is as cruel as a school which causes him to despair of being useful. Every civilized society is a differentiated society and leads its members on various paths to the fulfillment of their social tasks; it embodies hazards and restrictions. Only in a historical situation where suddenly an unforeseen number of occupational possibilities emerges — e.g., in a pioneer environment where everybody has a chance who can plow, build, and shoot, irrespective of whether he is able to read, write, and judge — can a school system afford to be unarticulated. In a more settled society, as ours now is, the ideal of social mobility must not be understood in the sense that all have to run along the same track toward the same final goal. Everyone can achieve the best for himself and his fellow men only when he has learned to master efficiently at least one of the many thousand tools which have to be handled in order to keep our complex social order intact.

Let us not deceive ourselves. It sounds nice to say: "Why shouldn't a salesman or police officer, a painter, a janitor, and perhaps finally every street cleaner have a college education? Would we then not have the ideal democracy?" What would we really have? We would have hundreds of thousands of people who dislike what they do because they think they had the right to expect something better; we would have a vanishing of good practical craftsmanship and of personal initiative, neither of which is learned from sitting on school benches; we would have more and more people waiting for help from the government, and if such help can no longer be provided by taxing the productive part of the population, some kind of a revolution.

Thank heaven, though the situation seems serious, there is no reason for despair in this country. But despair was the keynote of the conditions which prevailed in pre-Hitler Germany. And in a number of other countries the problem of an unemployed academic class has already brought about serious disturbances of the social equilibrium.[4]

Consequently, let us have a school system that helps people to like what they *can* do, because they know there is some dignity and reward in all work performed with devotion. But let us avoid the sort of inorganic and unnatural school which thrives on white collar prejudice, on inertia among educators, and on resentment of people who falsely believe they would be happier if we all were submerged in the gray mist of uniformity.

C. *Summary*

Our outline of a philosophy of secondary education is now completed. It has been in actuality a description of the human road toward maturity.

The following conditions must be fulfilled if we wish to arrive at the goal. As the matrix in which to embed all detailed knowledge and activities, we need a genuine culture of our emotions. Only if we are emotionally strong, but live at the same time in dynamic harmony with our affective life, can we co-operate joyfully with our society. Society and its various institutions easily become ends in themselves, however, or sink down below the standards of their most valuable members, unless the citizen possesses in addition to his social tendencies and duties a goodly endowment of liberal individualism. Hence the desire for co-operation, and the comfort that goes with it, must not be allowed to silence the inner voice of conviction, should a conflict arise between our conscience and the temporary will of governments, political parties, or power groups. The

---

[4] See in this respect Walter M. Kotschnig, *Unemployment in the Learned Professions*, London, Oxford University Press, 1937. The books by Seymour E. Harris have already been referred to in Chapter I.

perilous tendencies toward self-aggrandizement, inherent in all power groups, are encouraged by timidity and indifference on the part of the citizen. If the delicate balance between the rights of the individual and the rights of the collective is disturbed, then the brotherhood of free men changes into a life of suspicion and tyranny.

Our schools misunderstand their purpose, in short, if they believe they have to make the minds of the young ready for an obedient kind of citizenship. Non-conformity, provided it starts from worthy convictions and insights, may on occasion be the higher duty toward one's country and humanity.

But divergent convictions and insights cannot exist without being tempered by rational values. Rationality, in turn, can come about only as the result of man's mastery over the difficulties of his complex environment — and such mastery requires the mental virtues of persistence and the seeing of relationships. If we lived in a completely predetermined mechanical world we would not need such mental effort, nor would it be of any use. But neither would we be human beings. The world of man is still one of freedom, however limited this freedom may be by the forces of physical nature. Man has the chance to live productively if he behaves wisely, and to perish if he is ignorant or vicious. Reality is not something "given" to him, but something he has constantly to mold and remold in order to conquer it progressively.

This insight into the nature of reality, however, or this wisdom, grows not out of a theoretical and contemplative attitude; it requires the stimulus and test of action. Men can mature only if they have vigorous emotions which they can judge and guide by rational convictions, and they can have rational convictions only through the stimulus and test of action.

For such a full life, and also for the acquisition of self-respect, man needs an education which is to a degree general, but primarily liberal in character. This is an education toward wholeness. Far from being an amassing of information, it should help a person continually to enrich his spiritual and practical life through contact with those parts of the tradition and the strivings of mankind in which he is genuinely interested and from which he can profit.

Each of the qualities mentioned in this chapter is intimately related to all the others. Only in unity can they constitute the equipment that modern man needs to become truly adult, or to develop the degree of character of which he is capable.

The public education of modern countries is mass education. This is not only a necessity we have to accept but a blessing for which we have to be grateful. However, if mass education creates only a mass man absorbed in mass feelings and unable to maintain his individuality against leveling influence, then mass education is not the way toward civilization but toward its end. We need a school which, emotionally and intellectually, roots a person in the common experiences of his people and of humanity, but which also heightens, and makes him proud of, his individuality. For only the man who, together with a deep loyalty to his society, feels an equally deep loyalty to his self, can truly live *within*, and at the same time *for*, his fellow men.

CHAPTER FIVE

On the Education of Teachers

ANY THOROUGH DISCUSSION on education ends invariably in a reflection concerning the personality and capability of the teacher.

Let us sum up all the qualities the public demands from a desirable teacher. He, or she, should be sympathetic, tactful, morally blameless, and a citizen of such loyalty that even the most suspicious investigating committee could find no fault. However, he should also have a strong character and a critical mind free from prejudice. He should be an expert on education and psychology, well grounded in the subject matter he teaches, and a companion of his students in their extracurricular activities. He should teach Sunday school and lead in the men's Bible class. He should know how to handle parents, principals, superintendents, janitors, and school boards. Whatever the salary, if he is of male sex, he should be married, have several children, live in a respectable section of the town, and have a nice little library. Of the female teacher many communities demand that she leave marital joys to other women. As a compensation, she should deeply feel the delight which supposedly lies in educating other people's children.

But how find these paragons of virtue, knowledge, gentleness and thrift for a profession that in the United States comprises at present more than a million members?[1] Somewhere in his essays on *The American Scene* Henry James uses the masterful phrase: "an aching void." This is exactly what we sense when we discuss the problem of teachers, and the problem of the understanding of the teaching profession by the general public.

A paradox faces the teaching profession. On the one hand, teachers are of paramount importance. They cannot be expected alone to save a nation from the blunders of politicians, yet, through inefficiency, they can spoil its future and the happiness of its children. On the other hand, a teacher needs almost superhuman patience and love for youth in order not to become desperate in view of the endless repetition, testing, drill, paper work, and pettiness of his activities — all things which are characteristic especially of American schools where teachers often teach for years and years one and the same grade in one and the same subject. It is dangerous everywhere for the members of a profession to talk always to minors, to elicit responses and arguments which they know more or less beforehand, and to lack the friction with adults and the excitement of venture that make the life of an energetic man worth living.

As a result of this gap between responsibility and reward, it is impossible to find teachers of high quality for every school.

Hence, not only from the pupil's but also from the teacher's point of view we need a new type of school, full of life, variety, and changing responsibility; an institution which is worthy of an energetic person's devotion and is a challenge to the community.

We often hear that there must first be the good men before

---

[1] See *Teaching as a Career*, Bulletin No. 11, Federal Security Agency, Office of Education, 1947

there can be the good institution, but a statement of this sort is nothing but comfort in escape. If a society presents a challenging task and invites men and women to engage in it collectively, it will have the right people, whereas as isolated individuals distributed over wide areas of wasteland these same men and women have no chance to show their initiative. There never exist men on one side and institutions on the other; one has to add a third factor, namely the spirit of society. If it is weak, men and institutions fail to support each other; if it is strong, both enter into a dynamic whole and then we have the historical situation out of which brave social action ensues.

As things stand now, some vital factor seems to be lacking. Since the times of Pestalozzi, perhaps even since Comenius, the essential principles of a healthy education have been known; in some way, they have been taught to thousands and thousands of teachers. In every generation some people have experimented, and our psychological insight has increased. How, then, could one of the well-known pioneers of modern teaching, while looking back at his long career, declare that he could count on his fingers the schools which had really carried his ideas into practice? How can it be explained that today, even at public and private secondary schools with nation-wide reputations, one can observe instruction worse than it was fifty years ago at so-called old-fashioned European *lycées* and Gymnasiums? The teaching of science has probably improved; in the other fields one finds unevenness of quality. Is it because these old teachers of the classics were, on the whole, better scholars? They were. They had themselves attended a good secondary school and, consequently, did not need to use their university years for learning the rudiments.

But this is only part of the picture. The main reason is that young men and women who enter the teaching profession with high ideals after some years come back to their professors with a deep feeling of frustration. They carry on, because they have made their choice, but they see to it that as quickly as possible they become "school administrators." They are thus better paid and believe they enjoy a higher degree of human enrichment than in the classroom. However, the pillar of a nation's school system is not its administrators or its supervisors, but its teachers. Those who still have faith and enthusiasm are either the incorrigibly great teachers before whom we all should bow in gratefulness, or women who sublimate for the lack of a family. But the majority feel disillusioned, even those who carry the banner in spite of their institution's failure to challenge their talents to the fullest.

Thus in this, as in almost any other country, the schools remain backward institutions. If an industrial enterprise neglected the knowledge available for improvement to the same degree as schools do, it would be bankrupt within a few years.

But no situation is so hopeless that man cannot think about the principles that might direct constructive action. However distant the goal may be from present reality, let us contemplate the fundamental postulates on which to build the education of the teacher. If they cannot be fully materialized, at least we can try to avoid as much as possible discordant action stemming from sheer ignorance.

1. The Teacher as a Lover of Youth

The teacher on the elementary and secondary levels who expects that his satisfaction will come primarily from "professional" interests in the sense of technical skill and scholarly interest in a specific area of knowledge and research will sooner or later be disappointed.

Whoever has gone through the old secondary schools of Europe will remember with gratefulness some instructor who could just as well have been a professor at a good university. Some of them actually were. But he will also remember the tragic figures who suffered from an acute feeling of frustration and inferiority because of their failure to receive a university appointment. Being placed in an old and perhaps reputable school of a small town, they lacked the facilities of a big library and the exchange of ideas possible for the more privileged scholar — as is the case with many of our instructors at small colleges. At the same time, they did not perceive the springs of happiness from which they could have drawn had they developed a feeling of love and understanding for the youth entrusted to their guidance. Their ambition was to write a book or one more article on an obscure problem; it did not matter to them that their pupils also developed a feeling of frustration and inferiority.

In this country we sometimes go too far toward the other extreme. We seem to believe that the teacher's scholarly knowledge of his subject is unimportant in comparison with training in methods and psychology, which alone, however, do not make a good teacher. All three are necessary: the understanding of what one teaches, how one teaches, and whom one teaches.

Subject matter repeats itself in a teacher's work, however, even in that of a university professor with all his freedom. Of course, new books should always be read; deeper thinking and finer personalization of knowledge should always be the mark of a good schoolmaster. Nevertheless, the bulk of knowledge to be taught to sixteen- or seventeen-year-old boys and girls will remain largely the same, for adolescents are not yet engaged in research. That which changes every year are the "kids." For them the subject, which the teacher may be able to recite in his sleep, is young and fresh and perhaps even overwhelming; for them it has ever to be reorganized, new gates of entrance have to be opened, and new questions have to be answered.

Here primarily lies the inexhaustible source of vitality for the teacher. The motivation which causes him to look at every new class of pupils as at a new adventure and a new responsibility must come from a deep love for young people. If this is absent, a teacher's life is drudgery; if it is present, a teacher's life can be permanent rejuvenation.

2. *The Teacher as a Lover of People*

The teacher is responsible not only to his pupils. He is responsible also to their parents and to the nation. This responsibility cannot be fulfilled out of a merely legal or professional sense of obligation; it must be caused and molded by a profound sympathy with the life of people.

Just as the best instruction in educational psychology and methodology does not make a good teacher, unless he loves his children, so the best instruction in social science does not make him a friend and counselor of the parents unless he is himself part of the community.

Of course, this identification with people must not be interpreted in the sense of the teacher being the obedient servant of politicians, the school board, and those parents who are convinced that their beloved offspring are always right, whereas the school is always wrong. If we want to ruin the public school, let it be the instrument of petty politics and undiscriminating parents. To have a formula for what we mean we could use Rousseau's distinction between the *volonté de tous* and the *volonté générale*. The teacher should not follow the *volonté de tous*, or the will of everybody who happens to live in the neighborhood, but the will which results from the best in the co-operative and moral spirit of his nation.

Here emerges a crucial problem in the public life of the United States: What is the role of the teacher in the American community? Can he feel himself as the representative of the public will, if the public refuses to accept him as a citizen with the same political and social rights as the manufacturer, the grocer, the newspaper editor and the worker in the next plant? One of the most amazing of the contradictions in American democracy is that on the one hand there is continual reference to Jefferson's statements about the relationship between education and the survival of the republic, and on the other hand is the general feeling that the guidance and schooling of youth can be left to women or men who are not fitted for business.

American society has complacently indulged in a similar feeling with regard to public service in general. This service was not well paid, seemingly did not allow much room for initiative, and somehow it was the domain where "dirty politicians" had their hands. For these opinions, rooted in the country's past, and because of this past not even totally unjustified, the United States has to pay dearly, not only in billions of money but also in thousands of lives. Today, with this nation's being driven out of isolation, the public begins to realize the fault, as is proved by the strange coincidence of the foundation of schools for public administration and the activities of senatorial and other inquiring agencies which are a disgrace to the honest public servant.

The emergence and apparent public appeal of such voluntary associations as the National Citizens Commission for the

Public Schools proves that the light begins to dawn also with respect to the public service of the teachers. Of course, the revival of almost medieval forms of inquisition into the teacher's convictions, such as teachers' oaths, will not essentially improve our public school system. But honest co-operation between public-spirited citizens and teachers will.

3. The Teacher as a Guide toward Better Living

A teacher should be his pupils' guide not only toward more knowledge, but also toward better living. Of course, a mature understanding of the problems of modern individual and social life cannot be demanded from young people who just enter a vocation. Who, in this sense, is fully mature? But even a young teacher should look at life with a more developed mind than an adolescent. Then, should we not ask to what degree dormitory life in a typical college or teachers college — with all the advantages springing from communal living — may be too narrow and isolated for developing a young personality? College life today is too much regulated by prescribed courses, credits, and grades. It has little influx from the social and political events of a normal community where people have to earn their daily bread and are confronted with the changes of employment and unemployment; where old industries go down and new industries arise; where wealth and poverty, love and hatred, responsibility and vice clash. Some colleges have tried to plant their social studies in the local community, but the attempts of even these few have not always been welcomed locally. Were the respectable citizens afraid that the young teacher could learn too much about social inequality and decide to do something about it?

During the past years more and more people have recognized that there is too much listening and prescribed reading in our liberal arts colleges and too little room for personal initiative. Certainly the situation is not better in the typical teachers college. The shying away of the veterans from these institutions shows that they have little attraction to the more mature mind. The two-year course of the old normal school has been changed by stretching it across four years, but in spirit many institutions have remained the old "teachers seminaries."

4. Teaching and the Value of Inspiration

The teaching profession is an inspirational profession; consequently it needs inspired men and women. Our teachers colleges, however, have tended to keep up with the Joneses by aping as much as possible the coolness of the scientific method. While the scientist can be a well of inspiration, the person who imitates just his "method" and confuses the method for the total outlook toward life is a source either of dullness or of ridicule. With all the emphasis upon the teaching of psychology, testing, and methods of teaching a dozen subjects, the initiation of the student teacher into the cultural tradition is neglected. The great philosophies and religious systems through which man has gradually arrived at an understanding of himself, are mostly unknown. To many educators, what happened before John Dewey seems not worth noticing, as if Dewey himself could have formed his thought without, though partly in protest against, Plato, Hegel, Herbart, Darwin, and Marx.

Even Dewey is not really read and understood: only some of his pedagogical works are touched upon, his more comprehensive works being considered "too difficult." Thus some so-called students of Dewey can state later in a university graduate class that Dewey "believes in a personal God" whereas others say that according to Dewey "relativism" is the only answer. And they can argue that since we cannot know anything anyhow, we should ask ourselves whether it is desirable for man to think; he may just as well "not think." The people who utter this nonsense are not at all incapable of some philosophical discourse; they are even eager for it. But somehow, all they have to live on are half-digested, philosophical and culturally infantile phrases, defended in the name of "pragmatism," "relativism," some other kind of dogmatism, or in the name of "democracy" and "the American way of life."

How can people with that muddle in their heads arrive at any substantiated opinion about problems the solution of which determines not only their own philosophy and practice of teaching, but the survival of their country and its culture: problems such as the relation between freedom and authority, self-development and discipline, experience and tradition, self-expression and form, nationalism and internationalism, secularism and religion, individualism and collectivism, science and humanity?

Part of this neglect of the fundamentals of educational philosophy can be traced to two factors. One, that the teachers of teachers have learned somewhere that metaphysics is an obsolete and subjective discipline of thought. And since even the greatest ignoramus discovers sooner or later that the thorough discussion of any of the problems just mentioned enters into metaphysics, he simply puts them aside.

The second factor is that our public schools are established on the highly laudable principle of the separation between state and church. This means that denominational creeds do not belong in the public school, which in turn means that controversial issues of a world outlook or philosophy are hot irons, better to be kept at a distance because a fanatical priest or minister or atheist might complain. Thus the ideal of religious freedom, for which our ancestors in various Western countries have shed their blood, now makes of us cowards in conviction. We concentrate on "facts" and "methods" without ultimate directives; the only directive left is "democracy." But what makes democracy alive? Absence of faith?

We stated as a postulate that the teacher should inspire. But whence does the power of inspiration spring? First of all from a person's belief that his saying and doing have some general value. But there are other sources: a person's capacity to inspire springs also from his imaginative cooperation with worth-while associates. Imagination without worth-while associations would be empty; associations without imagination would produce nothing but a jumble of dull facts.

Now, the source of energy that kindles a person's imagination and produces associations lies mainly in a full life itself. But since, as we said, such fullness and richness cannot be expected in the experiences of young people, they have to be produced vicariously through acquaintance with the great treasures of imaginative creation, such as religion, literature, and the fine arts. Some kind of art every young teacher should try himself, not for the purpose of becoming a musician, or a painter, or a poet, but because, as in sport, only he can really appreciate another's performance who has somehow participated himself. But how much of this inspiration do our prospective teachers receive in the teachers colleges, liberal arts colleges, and universities?

5. The Art of Conveying

The teacher needs the art of conveying. This is not just a problem in methods of teaching. Nobody can convey effectively what he does not know thoroughly. Therefore, in a good institution for the training of teachers there should not be the artificial separation of subject matter and method; both should go hand in hand. For example, if in a teachers college the instructor in English literature has a class in Shakespeare, he should interpret his work in such a way that he sharpens the student's sensitivity for the art of revealing the inner beauty of literature. As long as we continue the separation of subject matter and method we shall remain in an artificial situation, with all kinds of specialists in methods occupying professorial positions in our teachers colleges, and the graduates becoming more and more uneducated. Thus by the emphasis on courses in method we may do the opposite of what we intend: we may prevent young people from becoming good conveyors of the values of civilization. In making this statement I do not join the chorus of these who believe that a teacher is "born" and does not need instruction in the art of instructing. Some of the so-called method courses may indeed be unnecessary, even harmful. Still, who can believe that a teacher can effectively meet his classes in a big public school by just reciting what he has learned in college?

Only after the art of teaching has been interpreted to the incipient teacher in combination with the active and vital acquisition of the subject matter itself, should methodology of teaching be given in special courses. Such courses should span two poles. One pole should be a thorough discussion of the theory of learning, not only psychologically, but also philosophically, i.e., in relation to the important theories of knowledge from Aristotle through the present. It is tragic to see how psychologists even in well-known university departments take up problems of the intellectual and ethical behavior of man without the faintest knowledge of a philosophical tradition that could help them set their experiments into a much more comprehensive context. This is not only the fault of modern psychological training; it is just as much the fault of the philosophy departments which during the past fifty years have practiced the art of self-isolation with unusual success.

It is time that the centrifugal development which has torn the humanities and social sciences apart be replaced by a new integration. There is hardly a field of study and practice more in need of and at the same time so well fitted for that purpose as education. In a deeper sense, it cannot be understood without the help of philosophy, psychology, sociology, and history.

The other pole should be observation, experimentation, and the application of theory in direct contact with children, not in a casual way, but extended over a period long enough to make possible real familiarity with the learning process and behavior of young children and adolescents.

6. *The Teacher as a Specialist*

The teacher must be a specialist. Even if he teaches in the elementary grades where according to modern principles there is no strong articulation of subject matter, he or, in this case, she has to be trained as a specialist. With respect to psychological and pedagogical problems the teacher of the very young pupil needs perhaps more professional preparation than the teacher of subject matter in a higher grade who may delude himself into believing that he has done enough when normally gifted boys and girls pass his examinations. Certainly, in the old, so-called humanist tradition, the learned teacher of Greek and Latin looked down upon the little grade-school teacher who, in reality, did not teach more and often did not know more than the bare rudiments of reading, writing, and arithmetic. With the recognition of the specific complexities of childhood, and the rise of the prestige of the public schools in democratic societies, this has changed or, to speak more carefully, is beginning to change. Even in the older European countries, despite the opposition of the secondary schools, there is a growing tendency toward a unity within the teaching profession.

As everywhere, the consolidation of a profession (which, with respect to the teachers of the United States, is of rather late date) goes hand in hand with the establishment of standards and entrance requirements. The early medieval universities established their reputation by insisting vigorously on definite rites in examinations and procedures of appointment. But when, at the end of the Middle Ages, the professors relaxed these rules, their institutions went down. To be sure, the laxity and corruption in the examination system of this period was but a part of the general disintegration of the medieval guild society and its social and spiritual foundations. However, all historical studies of professions and their preparations point to the fact that without a definite formalism and rigidity in the procedure of selection and appointment, corruption and decay are bound to occur.

There is the reverse danger too. We find it in all nations with a large officialdom and rigid bureaucracy — in nations which the United States has now joined — the danger of inflexibility and fear of new blood. Such a result is deplorable in the teaching profession. For this profession must be sensitive to intellectual and social changes, and should be open to persons of unusual character and experience even if they have not received the regular professional training.

This would be impossible with respect to the physician, the lawyer, and the engineer, but is, in certain cases, possible with the teacher, just as it is possible in public administration. As already indicated, the slow development of definite standards for the work in schools is due to the irresponsible opinion that dealing with children is something of lesser importance. Evidence of this irresponsibility is the fact that historians of modern nations have given no attention to the development of the educational system of their countries. The ways by which a people tries to transmit its ideas and ideals to the oncoming generations seemed to the historian of no importance. But there may also have been a positive reason for the neglect of rigid standards in the teaching profession. Wise people know that a young person learns most from contact with men and women in whom he feels kindness and a wealth of experience. This vicarious participation of the less mature in a more mature life is probably the greatest blessing in human development. This vital truth seems to have been somewhat forgotten.

The attraction which a young person may feel to older men and women is not necessarily caused by their extended professional training. Unspoiled young people possess fine sensitiveness for unobtrusive, genuine quality in whatever field it may prove itself. Hence it would be a pity beyond measure if our new school deprived itself of the participation of such superior personalities, just as it is hardly understandable that some of our Protestant churches do not invite the co-operation of outstanding men and women in their services, but leave the weekly sermon exclusively to ministers who, as all human beings, cannot always present to their congregations new bouquets of wisdom.

Our ideal school will also have to struggle with the difficult problem that confronts the vocational schools in every country: that is, how to find the instructor who combines impressive technical skill with the humanistic quality and methodical art of a good teacher. Often if the technical knowledge is adequate, the pedagogical quality is not, and vice versa. It is particularly in this area where our teachers colleges are least efficient and least equipped. Therefore, especially for the education of our young workers, let us recruit men and women even without specific pedagogical preparation, provided they can by their vigorous personalities benefit our youth and the nation.

Whatever the special field of a teacher, one condition should be fulfilled, granted that for a mass profession it may seem almost too high an ideal. Although the teacher cannot be a "creative" mathematician, scientist, linguist, or artist in the strict sense — how many of our university professors are? — he should nevertheless have acquired a *sense of the creative process*. Of what use is a man who talks about horsemanship, and has never been on a horse? Yet thousands of teachers talk about science and have never projected themselves into the exciting situation of a great discoverer. Others speak about art and seem never to have felt the intensity of experience out of which the creative work of art arises, if only with the effect that they might have discovered the difference between the mind that creates and the mind that explains.

Today we have become modest with regard to the influence of the school and the teacher upon society. We know that education is more the determined than the determining factor in human culture. Yet, to a degree, it is both. For civilization is not a dead mass of material which can be moved like furniture from the house of the deceased into the house of the heirs. While passing from one generation to another, civilization changes its character according to the spirit of those who transmit. Transmission of values is not just a process of "handing down;" it is at the same time reinterpretation. It involves choice and selection: it is either continual renascence or it is nothing but a show and a burden. Thus the teacher, who is the transmitter, must also be the interpreter, the selective agent, the reviver and regenerator; otherwise he is not a blessing, but a curse to the younger generation. If he looks at the drama of civilization with lifeless eyes, if he does not feel as one of the actors in this perennial drama, how and what can his pupils learn from him?

CHAPTER SIX

Higher Education

1. *The Structure*

If our considerations with regard to the secondary level of education are correct, they should apply *mutatis mutandis* also to the higher level. For the essential conditions of human nature must be as valid with respect to a student in college as to an adolescent in high school. Undoubtedly, differences exist. But they are less important, because the high school pupil and the undergraduate in college are human beings who are still learning and growing.

Before concentrating on the college and university, let us first take a somewhat wider view and find out what should happen to the graduates of our ideal high school who did not attend the humanist and scientific divisions.

In all likelihood the pupils of the fifth division, those who did not show any particular ability justifying a special schooling, will join the large numbers of practical and relatively unskilled workers who vote as citizens, and on whose work the welfare of our whole society rests. Let us hope that we have forms of adult education, broad enough in scope and related to their interests and capacities, so as to make it possible for them to enrich their lives, improve their working conditions, and participate productively in the social and political responsibilities of the community. We will speak of this problem in our next chapter.

What will happen to the boys and girls of our fourth, the artisans', division? Many of them will also be practically occupied, preferring apprenticeship and the ventures of life to school benches, and perhaps arriving that way at better positions than their more school-minded comrades. They will be qualified carpenters on whom we can rely for making or repairing a good piece of furniture or the roof of our house; they may be the watchmakers to whom we can entrust a good piece of craftsmanship cherished by our family, or the mechanics who give us a feeling of confidence when they tell us something about our car. Others may be designers and help our various industries to combine utility with some beauty. Some will become artists in their own right. But many will also feel the desire to combine their vocational plans with related fields of study and to have, at the same time, the advantage of a more extended general education. So they will perhaps attend a two-year junior or "community" college or an advanced vocational school in agriculture, nursing, the fine arts, mechanical engineering, business, etc.

There they will meet friends from all the various divisions of their former high school. Some, coming from the fifth division, will in the meantime have developed higher ambitions in connection with a clearly grasped and stimulating life purpose. Some may have arrived from the divisions of the humanities and the sciences because they have lost their pleasure in theory or cannot afford the expenses of a protracted professional training. And surely, a good number of the students from the third division, that of the young executives and businessmen, will wish to prepare themselves beyond their high school knowledge for those many branches of modern business which do not necessarily demand college graduates but nevertheless require a developed capacity of thinking, understanding, and communicating with other people.

For all these reasons the junior colleges have become popular. It is one of the good sides of the *Report of the President's Commission on Higher Education* of the year 1947 that its authors look with favor at the terminal junior college. But it is one of the sad sides of the actual picture of American higher schooling that the astonishing growth of the junior or community college (from about 50 to about 600) during the years 1920-1940 has been retarded considerably during the last seven years. Only about 10 per cent of students enrolled in higher institutions now attend junior colleges. The percentage should be much higher, thus taking away from the four-year theoretical colleges the more practically gifted youth who should not wait too long before arriving at an adequate position which in turn makes it easier for parents as well as for the nation as a whole to provide the already frightening expenses for advanced studies.[1]

But the lure of prolonged studies and an academic title seems to be overwhelming even in a country which is so prone to denounce the "armchair scholar" in his famous "ivory tower."

The junior colleges should vary greatly according to the social conditions of the particular area, whether industrial or agricultural, thinly or densely settled, whether in need of men who understand something of raw materials or of refined processes. But despite all variations, they should have certain tasks in common. There will probably be a business department for boys, and departments of domestic arts, nursing, advanced secretarial work, and hygiene for

---

[1] See in this context James Bryant Conant's article "The Community College" in *The Wiley Bulletin,* Fall 1950.

girls, since these occupations are needed everywhere. In addition, all junior colleges should have a good department of general education, which is not just an appendage to the technical departments as in many of our institutes of technology, but interacts most closely with all the other divisions of the institution.

Both teachers and students in the junior colleges will not look with envy and resentment at the traditional institutions of higher education and, out of false ambition, attempt to raise their alma mater to a four-year liberal arts college. For the junior colleges should be advanced schools in their own right, proud of enabling intelligent young people to enter into satisfying positions without the protracted and frustrating education often imposed upon youth by institutions which could do their four years' work better and more interestingly in half the time. We already have in this country four-year liberal colleges with underpaid teachers and mentally undernourished pupils. We also have good colleges for girls whose presidents still seem to believe that their students know of no other purpose in life than to do research in Romance philology or acquaint themselves with the complicated vocabulary of modern sex psychology. Instead of teaching in this aimless fashion, more and more open-minded men and women will prefer the clarity of purpose and the sound atmosphere of a good junior college. But it will, of course, be a real junior college, not one which hires the oldest teachers of the town's high school and pays them an additional few hundred dollars for offering on the college level the same physics which for the last thirty years they have taught to adolescents.

Through their interesting program junior colleges should attract young men and women who are anxious for a broader general education, but who want to see it integrated with a good preparation for more practical work. What else, after all, can be the purpose of a sound liberal education but to help a young person to find his purpose in life and to make it at the same time deep and wide? The more our junior colleges invite to their classrooms and laboratories young people who otherwise would have been forced to go to a four-year college, the better they serve the younger generation and the whole nation. For parents should not be compelled to pay for their children's education more than is necessary. In addition, a good and struggling junior college graduate can be of more worth to society than a mediocre and tired alumnus from a college of liberal arts.

All this involves the demand that the junior college should be a "terminal" institution, but not in the sense that a gifted youth should be prevented from passing over to a four-year liberal arts college and finally a graduate school if he feels the urge and capacity for more advanced and theoretical work. It should be "terminal" in the democratic and useful sense that a graduate of a junior college, after eight years of elementary, four years of secondary, and two years of higher training, has acquired some definite knowledge which allows him to apply with confidence for an interesting and rewarding position in the vocational life of his nation.

But let us now deal with higher education in the more academic context.

2. The Gentleman and the Scholar

Higher and secondary education are akin, though they live sometimes in a state of conflict. But exactly in such a state their close relationship becomes all the more obvious. In the past the professors in our colleges and universities could fancy being so far removed from the high school teacher that they did not need to bother about his troubles and failures. But today almost every college and university has or has had a committee concerned with the reform of studies. And the members of this committee inevitably discover that higher education cannot be separated from all the other forms of schooling, especially the high school. All educational institutions are affected by modern political and economic changes, by the crisis of our Western tradition, by the two world wars, and, last, but not least, by the increasingly critical attitude of youth toward the older generation. This attitude springs not only from the usual tension between generations in times of change — and when was ever a time without change? — but from the fact that the parents of today leave a hardly enviable heritage to the parents of tomorrow. Yet, it sometimes seems as if the concern about course credits and examinations, administration, new buildings, and new departments absorbs the time of many deans and professors to such a degree that only in words can they pay attention to the deeper problems of the modern university.

In order to understand the present historical situation, let us, in somewhat generalizing fashion, juxtapose two famous older types of university education. On the one hand we have the English type of character education in which the "gentleman ideal" prevailed for centuries over the scholarly ideal (which also existed); on the other hand we have the intellectual education of the continental universities, such as Paris in its various periods of flowering and Berlin in the nineteenth century, where the ideal of pure scholarship prevailed over the gentleman ideal (although again this also existed). Thus we discover on the university level the same difficulty in uniting fully the emotional-moral with the intellectual responsibilities of education which we laid open with respect to the secondary school. One could also use Oxford and Cambridge from the sixteenth to the nineteenth centuries as the symbol of *Humanitas,* and Paris and Berlin as the symbol of *Veritas.* To repeat, neither type ever existed in purity, and both no longer exist in their older historical forms. Oxford and Cambridge would rightly object to being called just "gentlemen's colleges," whereas the continental universities would maintain that, through providing knowledge, they have always intended to make a better man.

But let us first characterize the gentleman ideal by relating some passages from Cardinal Newman's *The Idea of a University,*[2] the beauty of which may serve as a proper excuse for the length of the quotation.

Today I have confined myself to saying that that training of the intellect which is best for the individual himself, best enables him to discharge his duties to society. The Philosopher, indeed, and the man of the world differ in their very notion, but the methods, by which they are respectively formed, are pretty much the same. The Philosopher has the same command of matters of thought, which the true citizen and gentleman has of matters of business and conduct. If then a practical end must be assigned to a University course, I say it is that of training good members of society. Its art is the art of social life, and its end is fitness for the world. It neither confines its views to particular professions on the one hand, nor creates heroes or inspires genius on the other. . . .

But a University training is the great ordinary means to a great but ordinary end; it aims at raising the intellectual tone of society, at cultivating the public mind, at purifying the national taste, at supplying true principles to popular enthusiasm and fixed aims to popular aspiration, at giving enlargement and sobriety to the ideas of the age, at facilitating the exercise of political power, and refining the intercourse of private life. It is the education which gives a man a clear conscious view of his own opinions and judgments, a truth in developing them, an eloquence in expressing them, and a force in urging them. It teaches him to see things as they are, to go right to the point, to disentangle a

---

[2] John Henry Cardinal Newman, *The Idea of a University,* Defined and Illustrated; first edition, 1852.

skein of thought, to detect what is sophistical, and to discard what is irrelevant. It prepares him to fill any post with credit, and to master any subject with facility. It shows him how to accommodate himself to others, how to throw himself into their state of mind, how to bring before them his own, how to influence them, how to come to an understanding with them, how to bear with them. He is at home in any society, he has common ground with every class; he knows when to speak and when to be silent; he is able to converse, he is able to listen; he can ask a question pertinently, and gain a lesson seasonable, when he has nothing to impart himself; he is ever ready, yet never in the way; he is a pleasant companion, and a comrade you can depend upon; he knows when to be serious and when to trifle and he has a sure tact which enables him to trifle with gracefulness and to be serious with effect. He has the repose of a mind which lives in itself, while it lives in the world, and which has resources for its happiness at home when it cannot go abroad. He has a gift which serves him in public, and supports him in retirement, without which good fortune is but vulgar, and with which failure and disappointment have a charm. The art which tends to make a man all this, is in the object which it pursues as useful as the art of wealth or the art of health, though it is less susceptible of method, and less tangible, less certain, less complete in its result. . . .

Hence it is that it is almost a definition of a gentleman to say he is one who never inflicts pain. This description is both refined and, as far as it goes, accurate. He is mainly occupied in merely removing the obstacles which hinder the free and unembarrassed action of those about him; and he concurs with their movements rather than takes the initiative himself. . . .

He never speaks of himself except when compelled, never defends himself by a mere retort, he has no ears for slander or gossip, is scrupulous in imputing motives to those who interfere with him, and interprets everything for the best. He is never mean or little in his disputes, never takes unfair advantage, never mistakes personalities or sharp sayings for arguments, or insinuates evil which he dare not say out. From a longsighted prudence, he observes the maxim of the ancient sage, that we should ever conduct ourselves towards our enemy as if he were one day to be our friend. He has too much good sense to be affronted at insults, he is too well employed to remember injuries, and too indolent to bear malice. . . .

If he be an unbeliever, he will be too profound and large-minded to ridicule religion or to act against it; he is too wise to be a dogmatist or fanatic in his infidelity. He respects piety and devotion; he even supports institutions as venerable, beautiful, or useful, to which he does not assent; he honours the ministers of religion, and it contents him to decline its mysteries without assailing or denouncing them. He is a friend of religious toleration, and that, not only because his philosophy has taught him to look on all forms of faith with an impartial eye, but also from the gentleness and effeminacy of feeling, which is the attendant on civilization.

Not that he may not hold a religion too, in his own way, even when he is not a Christian. In that case his religion is one of imagination and sentiment; it is the embodiment of those ideas of the sublime, majestic, and beautiful, without which there can be no large philosophy. Sometimes he acknowledges the being of God, sometimes he invests an unknown principle or quality with the attributes of perfection. And this deduction of his reason, or creation of his fancy, he makes the occasion of such excellent thoughts, and the starting-point of so varied and systematic a teaching, that he even seems like a disciple of Christianity itself. From the very accuracy and steadiness of his logical powers he is able to see what sentiments are consistent in those who hold any religious doctrine at all, and he appears to others to feel and to hold a whole circle of theological truths, which exist in his mind no otherwise than as a number of deductions.

Up to about 1850 Oxford had been under the dominance of a gentry who had learned the unique art of living on privileges without losing a certain measure of decency and without too much offense to the populace. This gentry could create the free gentleman's type of Oxford and Cambridge because the responsible positions in the country were not yet professionalized in the modern sense of the word. In contrast to the continent, the gentry had successfully opposed the inclination of European governments to mold the sons of the upper classes into career bureaucrats. England enjoyed the degree of decentralization which permitted character, initiative, and skill in handling human relations to outflank the *expertise* of government officials and other professions. The apprenticeship idea was applied not only in the crafts but also in the more privileged occupations. A prospective lawyer, judge, or physician received his training in the office, the courthouse, or before the sickbed; the main requirement was that the candidate for more prominent positions have good breeding and a "liberal education" — which was different from mere book learning. For though Oxford and Cambridge, just as their recruiting centers of Eton, Harrow, and Winchester, had a lot of dull book learning, there always was something more to them. Eton had corporal punishment, discipline, and sport, besides classical education, for only the four together were supposed to "break" a boy into a Christian gentleman; and Oxford had a kind of club life intermixed with lectures and exercises, all nicely balanced so that there was not too much danger of falling into the abysses of intellectualism.

But when we speak, as is necessary, of Eton and Harrow in connection with Oxford and Cambridge, we may question to what degree they all brought up the robust and extrovert ruler of the colonies more than the somewhat introvert and sensitive gentleman Cardinal Newman had in mind. As a matter of fact, English literature has many descriptions of the finest boys suffering from the severity of the masters and the cruelty of the older students.

In 1861, Herbert Spencer, in his treatise *Education: Intellectual, Moral, Physical*, attacked the prevailing harshness, then presumed to be the right preparation for the life of adults, in the following words:

Of this nature is the plea put in by some for the rough treatment experienced by boys at our public schools; where, as it is said, they are introduced to a miniature world whose hardships prepare them for those of the real world. It must be admitted that the plea has some force; but it is a very insufficient plea.

For whereas domestic and school discipline, though they should not be *much* better than the discipline of adult life, should be *somewhat* better; the discipline which boys meet with at Eton, Winchester, Harrow, etc., is worse than that of adult life — more unjust and cruel. Instead of being an aid to human progress which all culture should be, the culture of our public schools, by accustoming boys to a despotic form of government and an intercourse regulated by brute force, tends to fit them for a lower state of society than that which exists. And chiefly recruited as our legislature is from among those who are brought up at such schools, this barbarizing influence becomes a hindrance to national progress.

Yet Spencer was one-sided. Since history likes to proceed in contrasts it was inevitable that, as a representative of the new technically minded middle class, he would ridicule the classical studies and attack the monopolistic character of the English collegiate system. However, this system served a kind of aristocracy which knew it could maintain its power only if it risked its youth in order to make men out of them. The victims breaking down under the rigid discipline of Eton and Harrow were perhaps not too high a price paid by the English nation for building up its empire — provided one believes in the advantage of having an empire.

Of course, a school system alone does not mold the leaders of a nation. Family background, tradition, political environment, and sound outlets for youthful activity are probably more important. Perhaps, in the historical situation of the eighteenth and nineteenth centuries England would have been just as successful with another kind of school than Eton and Oxford. But the least that can be said against Spencer's attack is that the English system of collegiate education, despite all its defects, represents the most successful and lasting type of an elite-training developed by any modern Western nation.

And this ought to make us pause and think.

How different are the background and genesis of the German universities of the nineteenth century which presented to their contemporaries the most scholarly type of higher learning! They owed their intellectual and partly even their physical existence to two great movements of thought, the Enlightenment (or the period of Rationalism) of the eighteenth century and the movement of idealist Romanticism of the nineteenth century.

The Enlightenment concept of higher studies represented the protest of a new secular society against the domination of the universities by the theological faculties. Both in France and in Germany the advocates of the Enlightenment set the practical and social role of knowledge against the Catholic and Protestant tradition of religious transcendentalism. Important and productive though this opposition was, it failed to offer a comprehensive and integrating philosophy of higher education as a substitute for the lost unity which had existed under the guidance of the theological faculties. Under the influence of enlightened utilitarianism, higher education during the eighteenth century lost its universality; the universities became, or were in danger of becoming, a bundle of faculties each of them pursuing its own professional goal without co-operating with the others. In addition to the universities there existed the scholarly Academies. But though they were associations of great importance for the national and international intellectual life of Europe, they also were unable to provide a unifying philosophy of higher education. Against all this atomistic secularism — similar to what we have now — the idealists and romanticists of the German school of thought demanded a new organic and organizing idea which, of necessity, could not be content with mere externals but required a deeper principle of unification.

Seen from a large historical point of view, the University of Berlin, which was leading in the development of the new romantic-idealist concept of higher studies, is perhaps not more than an episode — not only because it is now destroyed and, as far as it still exists, under Russian control, but also because it represented too exalted an ideal to become of lasting influence in a world of rising empiricism and a world of cruel political realities.

Germany, with its small absolutist principalities, did not, like England, permit many outlets for the intelligent man outside the privileged nobility, unless he wanted to become a theologian or a scholar. Thus most of the talented youth of Germany turned toward the contemplative sides of life. The idea of the University of Berlin, put into action by Wilhelm von Humboldt in 1809, was the result of an introvert culture. Before and during the period of planning, the great idealist thinkers of the nation such as Kant, Fichte, Schelling, Steffens, and Schleiermacher wrote profound essays about the cultural mission of the scholar, probably the most profound ever written on this topic except for the treatise by Cardinal Newman on *The Idea of a University*.

More or less all these thinkers were concerned with a new interpretation of the concept of truth. Though secular in quality, it contained large elements of religious spirituality taken over from the old theological tradition. Truth, according to this concept, is the link through which the human mind unites with that which is universally valid. To be sure, truth-seeking man cannot discover more than a small part of reality as a whole. But the most important experience in the search for truth is not so much the objective result as the search itself and the attitude which results from it, namely, the widening of the ego over into the totality of existence which, however weakly comprehended, is nevertheless felt.

Thus the scholar, despite his inevitable limitations, is considered the priest of truth, and the university the place where the talented youth of the nation are to be initiated into the wonders of mind and nature.

Schleiermacher, whose theological thought greatly influenced liberal theology in this country also, writes in his memorandum concerning the foundation of the University of Berlin:

Can we expect that this spirit of an inner unity of the universe comes to man while he is asleep? Can we expect that exactly the cultivation and progress of knowledge arise out of nothing, other than through continuous creation, like all life? . . . Here is the essential mission of the university. . . . It represents the transition between two periods, the period of adolescence when youth is given the foundation of knowledge and the methods of learning, and the period when mature man becomes creative, senses the beauty of systematic thought and expands its orbit through his own contribution. Hence the university is entrusted with the starting of a process, with the supervision of its first development. But this process is nothing less than a totally new attitude toward life. The business of the university is to plant the idea and ideal of Truth into the minds of noble youth already prepared for it by their previous training. The university must help them to master the contents and methods of research in that special field to which they wish to devote themselves. But whatever they do, it must become natural to them to contemplate the detail from a philosophical point of view; that is to say, instead of seeing the singular object of research in isolation they must learn to see it in conjunction with related problems of thought. They must be able to incorporate the part into the great universe of the Spirit and to understand how this universe works in every single act of thought. Only in this way can they gradually acquire the art of original research, discovery, and presentation.[3]

[3] A free translation from F. Schleiermacher's *Gelegentliche Gedanken über Universitäten*, Berlin, 1808. Edited by Edward Spranger in his book: *Uber das Wesen der Universität*, Leipzig, Felix Meiner, 1919, pp. 126 ff.

One easily detects in these sentences the desire of the romantic idealist to substitute the universality of scholarly thought for the catholicity of the Christian faith, which had been lost.

With amazing clarity Schleiermacher and his friends saw the danger inherent in the problem of the patronage of the universities, especially the danger in state centralization. They were all born in the age of absolutism which they disliked. On the other hand they had become disappointed at the tyranny which, under the guise of liberty and equality, the French Revolution had exercised over the universities and their scholars. But what agency other than the state existed in Prussia, and other German countries impoverished and defeated by Napoleon, for supporting a new university? Thus the scholars set their hope on a kind of government willing to serve the country by a liberal policy in matters of higher education. This hope was not entirely unjustified in the era when a great thinker and statesman such as Wilhelm von Humboldt was Secretary of State; it was sometimes frustrated in periods of reaction, and again revived under more favorable circumstances. If one considers the seemingly inevitable limitations of all earthly government one can say that the German universities before Hitler did not suffer more from outside interference than the universities in other countries, probably less. On the whole, during the nineteenth century they were extremely productive.

But as there are no longer the Oxford and Cambridge as they were before 1850, so there are no longer the German universities inspired by the ideals of romantic idealism.

Both the old English and German universities depended on a hierarchical society, and this society depended on them. The Oxford gentleman was too little concerned with the "rest" of the people, but before about 1830 the "rest" did not belong to the English society. The German scholar also was a sort of aristocrat, not by heredity, but by the distinction which intellectual pursuits and especially a university career carried with them in the older Germany. Up to the age of Bismarck, the majority of professors were more on the liberal than on the conservative side. But, as is everywhere the case with scholars immersed in their research, only a few became political fighters, except in the abortive revolutions of 1830 and 1848. Thus, the conservative-ecclesiastical alliance, which actually had ruled Germany for centuries, defended itself successfully against the threats of democratic liberalism. Finally, Bismarck's overwhelming national successes brought the universities well in line with the political system of the empire.

And let us not forget that, despite all social injustice to the majority of the people, the dons of Oxford and Cambridge and the German professors had a good time. They were well protected, and there was little interference to disturb their scholarly peace. Intellectual values were appreciated, not merely because they added to power and influence, but also because of the riches they brought to the mind. One read old and rare books in ancient languages, discussed philosophical problems, wrote profound essays — at Oxford in palatial, though not always comfortable dormitories; in Germany often in the ill-furnished single room of a poor student. Certainly, neither the rich at Oxford nor the poor at Berlin were philistine.

The mentality which allowed a particular group to have such feudal or priestly standards changed in the era of growing industrialism and competition. This did not happen overnight, because the new bourgeois of the second half of the nineteenth century adopted many of the older conservative attitudes. The change came when technical inventions, capitalistic production and speculation, and the conquest of political and educational influence by the large masses caused that fermentation of our society in the midst of which we still find ourselves all over the world. In part, at least, this fermentation was brought about not only by political and economic forces, but also by the new troublemakers right within the universities themselves, namely the scientists. They did not believe in Platonism, Hegelianism, and other cryptic speculations. To the horror of the fathers and the delight of the sons these scientists did not even believe in religion. When Hegel said, "The Truth is the Whole," they answered, "So what. Let us begin with the details and then talk about the Whole" — until in the course of time they forgot the Whole completely and had only the scattered details. For what?

Thus the universality of human aspects disappeared under the spell of the ideal of exact research. We now have more refrigerators, and also more bombs which can destroy them and their owners. And while we also have much better physicians, we have too the millions wounded by the bombs.

For the invention of refrigerators and the production and healing of war casualties, a long scientific training is needed: twelve years of pre-college education, four years of college, and often about four to six years of graduate training and professional apprenticeship. During this protracted race for expertship many break down, some from lack of vigor, others from lack of money. No wonder that little time remains for all these wonderfully unnecessary things on which the older gentleman and scholar throve — those things which united humanity not in jealous competition for the next patent, but in the pursuits which make educated, liberal, and humane men out of potential beasts.

With this fading of the spirit of liberal education it could come about that certain internationally known professors of Germany — and of other countries too — could feel inspired by such trash as Hitler's *Mein Kampf*, whereas men imbued in the humane tradition had to read only the first pages to be overcome by a feeling of nausea. The style alone was sufficient. But even some students of ancient and modern literature belonged to the admirers, proving that the most dignified objects of study have no power over a man with a disillusioned and desiccated soul.

The temptation of falling prey to a false gospel is particularly great if it presents itself in the cloak of an appealing absolute, offering a cheap substitute for lost values of universal character. Today such an absolute is patriotism in the form of nationalism, with its glorification of "the country." A country, at present, is much less the old *res publica* than the domain of a government. And since governments, in spite of all democratic constitutions, become more and more big centers of powers usurping everything that comes within their reach, it may happen that suddenly culture and education find themselves under bureaucratic control. At the end of the process the scholars who try to use the might of governments and party machines for their own profit may find themselves in the position of appointees who are dismissed if they refuse to obey. And education becomes nothing but an instrument of political indoctrination.

3. *The Present Scene*

It is in partial realization of all these dangers to human civilization that, as we have said, almost every college and university has instituted a reform committee. The whole picture represents a vague groping for some kind of integrating philosophy — from Thomism to Jeffersonianism and Jacksonianism. It is difficult to discover a genuine modern philosophy of higher education able to give our universities the same depth of convictions which Paris had in the scholastic period, Wittenberg and Leyden in the Protestant era, and Oxford and Berlin in times not long past.

As always, when the spirit is lacking, man relies too much on externals. We change the age level for the liberal arts college, we organize survey courses, or we build a department of specialists for general education into the college of liberal arts, hoping that we may thus keep humanism in a house in which it no longer feels at home.

Everywhere we believe in the blessings of expansion. We think we mobilize democracy by drawing as many people as possible into college. What we do not seem to realize is that in this way we make good education more and more expensive, and deprive the non-college block of influence and initiative. For with the eyes of everybody directed toward a college diploma it becomes increasingly hard to prove that a man without this piece of paper may be capable of leadership.

A sterile busyness — which is different from courageous activity — has crept into the colleges and universities. By necessity, in such an atmosphere every measure of better selection ends in the imposition on the student of a still greater number of external requirements. For whenever the sense for the fundamental criteria is lost, more quantity is mistaken for better quality. But this confusion drives the sensitive type of student, among which there may be the most creative and original thinkers, to the verge of cynicism, if not of despair and insanity. We have in many and generally the most ambitious institutions an unhealthy crowding of subjects; new demands are streaming in from all sides; and there are no directive principles to avoid jams and collisions. Advancement of the younger staff depends on the number and thickness of the books they write; so they have little time to learn to teach, listen, live, and to deepen their thought through action and quiet speculation. Students and instructors are drowned in waves of grades and examinations; even graduate students are treated like children who do not know what and how to study — and many men and women at the age of twenty-five and even thirty seem to like this treatment. All this is not just a fault of administration, but affects the whole collegiate atmosphere. Eventually it will deprive a nation, once pioneer, of originality and enterprise.

Since a student risks spoiling his record and losing his scholarship by venturing into an unknown field of knowledge, he will prefer to stay at home and be safe, which means he will choose only courses close to his specialty. This intimidation could be avoided if the students, at least the better ones, were given the chance to attend about one-fourth of their courses without the requirement of grades and examinations. If an instructor makes this proposal, his colleagues look at him as if he intended to overthrow the American Constitution. The same professors complain at the small spread of interests, and in order to remedy this deplorable situation and to enforce some kind of liberal or "general" education they set into motion a new machinery of regulations and course programs. The student, however, does not become more liberal that way. He just wonders why there is so much talk about academic freedom and a free society, when he feels so little of it.

All this creates in stronger minds a deep resentment, and in weaker minds intimidation and a desire for conformity, especially as there are teachers who become irritated if the student expresses an opinion different from theirs. In other words, exactly that group of people in whom intellectual and moral courage should be developed and out of whom the productive heretics ought to rise are trained in voluntary acceptance of an immature state of thinking and living, though they are at the level of physical maturity.

Of course, some students would abuse their freedom. But what does it matter if the rest learn how to use it? American college youth are excellent material. Is it necessary that the desire for efficiency and immediate control of result nip in the bud the development of youth who would like to do better than their parents?

There is little time for the ripening of a true academic spirit in this atmosphere. Much of the enthusiasm of instructors who would like to see more freedom and elasticity gets bogged down in discussions about courses and credits. How can it be otherwise if the sense for the relationship of a subject to the deeper meaning of academic studies is lost, and if no time is left for the students themselves to discover this meaning through their own work and contemplation? It adds to the difficulty that, in consequence of the failure of so many high schools to prepare their pupils sufficiently for advanced studies, the college has to teach a host of typical secondary school subjects: ancient and modern languages, the elements of mathematics and the sciences, survey courses in history, even the rudiments of English composition — and all this after twelve years of schooling! For what have they been used?

From the other end the graduate schools impinge upon the four years available for the liberal arts college. Whereas the most productive scientists have generally a fine understanding for the cultural value of the *études désintéressées,* the minor specialists in the graduate departments fail to see that a broad general training helps their students even in a thorough and comprehensive understanding of their technical subjects. Rather than wanting the student to be more mature, they want him to be technically more advanced. However, their impatience is partly justified, for if the high school were better, the college could do both in conjunction: provide an advanced liberal training and connect with it more specialized knowledge.

But there is yet another reason for impatience. Why are the brave old defenders of the liberal arts so incapable of abandoning the idea that liberal values are attached only to a certain number of subjects? Why must a field be the more praiseworthy the more distant it is from application? Why do they not see that a liberal education thrives on the spirit in which things are taught much more than on the matter?

Of course there are limitations, or conditioning factors, in any liberal education.

The student must be motivated to think in relationships, not just to learn historical facts or mathematical formulas. Also, the subject must appear in a context which allows transfer of intellectual experience into wider areas of human and natural life. Furthermore, the various subjects must be interrelated in the sense that they complement each other. This must be understood not only materially, as a course in chemistry may complement a course in biology, or a course in French literature a course in French history. It must be understood also in a deeper human sense. For example, a course in philosophy or economics, or in the history of the fine arts, may be of great value to an engineer because otherwise his mind may get drowned under blueprints and calculations and lose contact with the freer interests of mankind.

Co-operation between liberal and professional education is necessary also for the following reason. Every profession roots deeply in the basic experiences of mankind, and it withers when these roots are not kept alive. The jurist who is ignorant of, or does not bother about, the meaning of ethics, justice, and government is with respect to his value for society below the level of a good mechanic. For a good mechanic is useful, whereas a sociologically and philosophically ignorant judge is a danger. What is true of the jurist holds true of all the other professions, of medicine, theology, education, government, engineering. The purposes of liberal and of professional education do not run parallel, or in chronological sequence; in a civilized person and society they should merge.

4. *The Search for Synthesis*

But how can we rededicate higher education to its proper place in modern civilization?

The answer can come only from the realization of the fundamental historical fact that the survival of a civilization depends on its capacity to combine courageous interest in new movements appearing in thought and society with a thorough respect for that which is great in the tradition. This respect is not at all identical with slavish imitation and conservation; rather it is an awareness of the fact that the higher a building, the more solid must be its foundation. Certainly, not everything which belongs to the past can serve as foundation. If the beams are decayed and the stones are corroded they must be thrown away and replaced by new ones.

If in the light of these reflections we examine once more the past, we will find that both old Oxford and the old continental universities contained, apart from the useless and even dangerous qualities, certain elements which we cannot allow to disappear without wrecking the whole edifice of our civilization.

The obsolete part in the Oxford gentleman ideal was its connection with the prejudices of caste and heredity. To-day, we no longer want to restrict the privilege of an all-round education to the scions of a few families a considerable part of whom may be inferior in abilities to those of more humble origin. Yet, there remain such values as harmony between intellect, character, and body, ease in behavior combined with energy, and the recognition that leadership is not only privilege, but also service and hardship.

The time of the old aristocrats is gone. And rightly so, because too many of them failed to live according to their own professed ideals; they became a parasitical element. Today we need men who feel with their people and who make articulate its often inarticulate longings. Though of the people and with the people, they must be men who can weigh the passions and demands arising in immediate situations against the more permanent demands of humanity; they must have taste and judgment with respect to human affairs; they must have the kind of inner freedom which makes them capable of opposing mere whims of the populace. And knowing that their work depends on an enlightened citizenry they will do whatever they can for the improvement of its moral and intellectual standard.

But here is the difficulty for the modern college. In earlier times, the gentleman was mainly a product of "good breeding." The philosopher John Locke, in his *Some Thoughts on Education* written at the end of the seventeenth century, tells us eloquently the conditions of this breeding: wealth and health in the family, friends from the same protected environment, good books, but no book learning, and a gentleman tutor who knows how to mix rightly kindness and severity — in other words, not scholarship, but character education. All this had to be built into the framework of a

Christian faith which, though already conventional, nevertheless guaranteed a certain degree of mental and moral stability.

Locke does not dwell on college education. In accordance with modern psychology he would have said that the ground for a gentleman must be laid at home and in his childhood; if these conditions are not given, a college may well produce a learned ass or a learned rascal. Perhaps Locke would not even have protested if somebody had stated that the gentleman grows in spite of Eton and Oxford.

Thus we admit frankly the limitations of our big universities with respect to the realization of the gentleman ideal. Even a good high school has greater possibilities because there the teacher is often in closer contact with the student, and the program can be more in keeping with the development of character than the college program, which, of necessity, is primarily intellectual.

There are, however, a great number of opportunities for the cultivation of the emotional life also in colleges. Many of the features demanded for our ideal new high school are potentially existent, often also materialized, in our better colleges. As a matter of fact, the campus with its various houses, the generally more fortunate location, the existence of art and music departments, gives the college advantages in terms of activities, exhibits and concerts rarely shared by other institutions. Students and younger professors often consider the art museum and the music building an integral part of their own inner education, though they are neither art historians nor professional musicologists.

There is college sport. But it must become the sport of all, not only of the men's football team or the girls' hockey club. Sport is the only part of college life where compulsion ought to be applied, for bodies which still grow must not be allowed to lead a merely sedentary life. And there are, in the Anglo-Saxon countries, the houses — for those, of course, who can afford to live in them. They ought not to be just dormitories, but centers of social intercourse, of discussion, of good amateur art performed by the students and teachers themselves, and, last but not least, of hospitality extended to the youth of the town who are not privileged to go to college. In how many houses of the colleges of the United States is this done? And yet it is the minimum of what college youth ought to pay back to the nation for the privileges they receive.

Contacts like these could also help to awaken a sense of social responsibility in the student. It is somehow difficult to understand, yet it is the rule, that by far the largest majority of students manage to live for four years in a city or town, often a small one, without the slightest interest in the local people and their affairs. But the suggestion that the college ought to be part of the community, not so much for the community as for the students, is often answered by the helpless question, "How can it be done?" As if co-operation and the discovery of common interests could arise without personal interest and contact!

How often does one see college students go out and help after a snowstorm, a flood, or in the pressure of a harvest? When do they help a poor community build a playground in one of the neglected districts? Perhaps in such activities they might learn more about sociology, government, psychology, and education than in merely theoretical or observational courses; in addition, the majority of young Americans would like to participate in them. But, with few exceptions, and these usually in emergencies, the professors frown: How can we grade and credit this kind of work? How can we make up for lost hours? Thus the work remains undone, and with it not only the job of continual democratization of the nation, but also the education of the student toward a fully developed personality. For such a personality can grow only in an atmosphere of concerted social action.

But the action must be combined with perspective; mere activity, however good, does not make a superior person. Therefore students must be acquainted with those sources of human thought from which mankind has derived its standards of human excellence; some of the great religious, philosophical, or literary documents must become their personal property still more than is possible at high school age. It makes no great difference how many and which of these documents will stay with a man or woman through life. The main thing is that they become inner companions with whom a person convenes in hours of crisis and hours of joy, and in whose company one can never be completely lonely.

Again this absorption of great thought into one's own personality needs time; it can never be a matter of hurried reading, squeezed like a luxury in between the assumedly more important technical courses. Nor must this kind of work be harassed by the fear of grades. Culture cannot be produced on the assembly line, and it is too precious to be measured. There is seeming waste in all things which belong to the soul; but if there is no waste there is likely to be no soul. Hence, efficiency brought to perfection means man pushed into decay. People who do not understand this are dangerous everywhere, but most of all in education.

With these considerations concerning the growth of a free and truly cultured gentleman we have already arrived at the other part of the university tradition which must be carried over into the future: the ideal of scholarship, or the demand incumbent upon the seekers of knowledge to combine the necessary concentration on a specific subject with a philosophical aspect of the whole. The fact that this concept of the whole is scientifically undefinable does not deny its significance. Like all great cultural visions, such as dignity, love, and devotion, it indicates a "direction toward." Without such direction the means become ends, and a civilization becomes self-centered and mechanical.

It is needless to state expressly that these directions are not static or exempt from continual scrutiny and revision in the light of new experiences. But all depends on whether this examination is done with a sense of respect and responsibility, or with an infantile lust for tearing down everything intangible because it cannot be subjected to the "scientific method." No doubt, this lust existed and still exists. But it did not exist at the time when the exact sciences had to blast their way against the dogmatic resistance of theologians. Men such as Galileo or Newton were deeply philosophical. The demon of anti-philosophical dogmatism arose during the nineteenth century when the directors of the laboratories thought that only three or four more problems had to be solved in order to eradicate definitely such superstitions as religion and metaphysics. And today, despite the disillusion of the disillusioners, we still have teachers who consider it their duty to create in their disciples a kind of spiritual agoraphobia. In the long run they will clarify our thinking much less than they will contribute to the general desiccation of imagination; a desiccation which shows in the lack of inspiring ideals and plans in our national and international politics.

But what can we do in order to restore the philosophical tradition of scholarship as it was alive in all creative periods of civilization?

Naturally, one turns first toward the philosophical faculties, only to realize soon that he does not find there "the hills from whence cometh my help." When whole generations began to lose faith in the power of the human mind to discover a universal meaning behind the details of life, the philosophers also became afraid of intellectual courage and tried to prove their respectability by surrendering to a narrow positivist spirit. Also, they forgot that a civilization cannot live on description, analysis, and accuracy alone, but needs intuition, vision, and, heretical though it may sound, a utopia. Reason, the great propeller of progress, is more than a timid logic; it is total, not merely partial, mobilization of the mind.

Always when men become too uncertain of themselves they lose their attractiveness. So it happened with the philosophers. And as always, the feeling of losing ground was accompanied by false defense attitudes. Thus the typical department of philosophy scoffed at such emerging interests as sociology, psychology, and education. Instead of keeping these new disciplines of thought within its motherly orbit, it allowed them to go their own way, or even pushed them aside, depriving itself of a rare opportunity to combine speculative and historical thought with experimentalism, application, and actuality. The new departments in turn felt no obligation to build their teaching and research into the matrix of a broader philosophical framework which they did not trust — though often they did not know anything about it. The result has been that they spent time repeating in newfangled technical terms, and after many costly detours, what the great philosophers had known and stated for many centuries.

Some universities, especially the European centers of learning, tried to preserve the philosophical tradition by compulsion: no graduation and final diploma without at least an oral examination in philosophy! But this examination became a fake just like the examinations in religion at other places. The serious professors of philosophy themselves recommended their abolition, just as serious theologians in this country advocated the abolition of compulsory chapel. After all, what is the use of forcing a prospective lawyer, biologist, or engineer into one or two courses in philosophy after the philosophical spirit in the academic studies as a whole has evaporated? Does a man whose mind is occupied with the acquisition of special knowledge become philosophical if he listens reluctantly to a course on Locke or Kant? We all know how slowly we learn and how swiftly we forget disconnected knowledge.

There is, however, some hope that the student's urge for seeing the relationships and not only the parts of knowledge can be awakened by philosophical or historical chairs planted in individual departments, as has been done in recent times by bigger universities. They have chairs for the philosophy or history of science, law, government, education, etc. The teachers in these positions are not remote from the specialists and they derive the objects of their research out of the area in which the student is working. If they understand how to show him the path that connects his particular segment with the universe of knowledge, they can be the rescuers of the spirit of total inquiry which is drowning in our universities. However, by no means could they make the philosophical departments unnecessary, for somewhere the basic theories such as logic, theory of knowledge, ethics, and metaphysics must be cultivated, and somewhere must be the final integration. But with a system of liaison between the individual departments and the faculty of general philosophy the spirit of universality may be gradually renewed, this time no longer on a romantic-idealist level away from experimental research, but on a plane where speculation and empiricism may happily meet.

Yet, it cannot be repeated sufficiently that all this will be an idle dream without the help of *all* professors of a university, including the scientists and specialists. If the whole field is dry and barren, even the few plants which might take root will be blown away sooner or later.

5. *What Should the Professor Profess?*

With what kind of mental attitude should the academic teacher be provided? What deeper sort of knowledge should he profess in order to deserve his title as "professor"?

When, years ago, the students of one of the Harvard houses invited me, together with some other teachers, to talk to them about the aim of academic studies, I was told by a young hearer that he still had not understood what we were talking about. So I asked him to turn around and look at the Harvard shield on one of the walls, with the word *Veritas* in its center. "What can I do with that one word?" asked the student.

I walked home with him and tried to explain what *Veritas* meant to me: the foundation, the goal, and the essence of a scholarly life, and of any free civilization worth living in and striving for. *Veritas* is not only an intellectual abstraction, nor is it solely a moral obligation. It also has a profoundly pragmatic value. For as long as a man pursues the goal of *Veritas* he will always be closer to reality than the one who does not. Of course, often it may seem to be more comfortable to remain in the fog. Always when men and nations despair of their capacity to master reality, they desert and persecute the truth-seeker, and follow the lure of lie and prejudice. For lie and prejudice are nothing but an attempt to escape the stern majesty of the laws of life. But in the long run the deserters cheat themselves; they are like drunkards who think that intoxication is a remedy against the pressure of facts.

When a searching man sees how the people around him cherish falsehood he is desperately lonely, and sometimes he may doubt whether he alone has the right to feel closer to the truth than the rest. Who knows with what seductive ghosts and demons the martyrs of *Veritas* had to struggle in their dark prisons before they decided to drink serenely from the cup of hemlock or to climb on the stake?

But the courage of fighting lies for the sake of truth has deeper roots than the mere desire for use and effectiveness. The real thinker always feels that the particular verity in which he believes is but a part of a greater unity. Whether or not he may be aware of it philosophically, he thrives on the feeling that in every bit of a new truth a greater and deeper truth is revealed. Every experience and every experiment of significance transcend themselves; though they are only a small segment of reality, they always point beyond the immediate to a great universe of meaning.

Who will ever embrace this universe? For we all "see through a glass, darkly," and we "know in part." But even though, unlike St. Paul, we may not dare hope ever to see "face to face," we nevertheless feel ourselves as links in the endless chain of evolution toward *more* truth, *more* reality, and *more* freedom.

Thus behind all the work done in our universities lies a metaphysics, both true and real, though hidden to some who, by a misunderstood concept of intellectual exactness, have lost the courage of imagination. This metaphysics says that the mind of man, by a mystery we are unable to explain, participates in a higher rational order which represents the unity of principles and laws as against the chaos of merely fugitive appearances and desires. The disciples of Plato and

St. John called it the "Logos" or "The Word," and believed
that by it they expressed the first and ultimate reality. But
it makes no difference whether we have this kind of faith
or whether we believe with Kant and the critical philosophers that the ultimate character of existence is veiled to
the human mind, because man can do no more than order
his impressions and ideas within his own narrow boundaries
of understanding. In both cases the scholar receives his
inspiration and dignity from his search for an ever-extending
universe of truth. Behind the magic of accidents he sets the
vision of a rational order.

This is the idea of *Veritas* which retains its value irrespective of whether, like the founders of Harvard College,
we hope it serves *Christo et Ecclesiae,* or whether we believe
in an idealistic philosophy, or whether we are modern
"naturalists" and skeptical about metaphysics. Wherever
men devoted to *Veritas* assemble, there is "Ecclesia," and by
this term the Athenians originally meant the assembly of
free men in council.

One of the fundamental problems of civilization is whether
the professional scholar believes he fulfills his cultural mission by trying to solve one or the other problem in isolation,
or whether each step forward in his knowledge will also be
a step forward in reverence before the great miracle of
the universe. In the first case scholarship will lead us into
helpless relativism, and science will make man the slave of
his own technology; in the second case it will help us toward
a new view of life in which the fallacious contrast between
intellectual search and comprehensive faith will disappear.

Then — and only then — will systematic knowledge contribute to the unity of civilization. It is an error to think
that this unity will come from weaving together more and
more threads which flutter loose on the surface of human

society, or from speedier forms of communication, or from
an international auxiliary language, however desirable the
latter may be. Certainly, organization and scientific exactness are needed, but unless mankind feels bound together
by its consciousness of a deeper order, external organization
will constantly be broken by centrifugal powers.

In advanced countries we are rightly proud of the separation between state and church. This separation was historically necessary. But unfortunately, it was not a real
separation. Rather it has turned over into a rivalry between
the spiritual and the political forces of mankind, the latter
being represented most effectively by the modern nation-
state, and often supported by churches in the false belief
that in this way they may support their own position. But
in the competition the nation-state has always won, and
as it is with religion, so will it be with scholarship. However widespread and international scholarly organizations
may become, they will be dispersed in future conflicts between countries and political systems just as easily as they
were broken up at the beginning of the last great wars. As
a matter of fact, the resistance against the tyranny of
governments has come not from "experts." Resistance came
from men and women who had not just a lot of little
truths, but felt somewhere the voice of *Veritas* to which so
many statesmen and university professors had become deaf.

In comparison to this voice, the gentleman ideal which we
stated as the first necessary directive in the philosophy of
higher education seems trivial. This would be so if one
conceived of it in the colloquial sense, designating nothing
but a man who knows how to behave in polite society and
who has certain standards of decency, especially in the
intercourse with people on whose judgment he lays value.

But if standards of decency are followed not just for

external decorum, and if we look deeper into the tradition of the gentleman ideal, we discover the close affinity between the Anglo-Saxon and the Continental concepts of the university. Both represent different accentuations of one and the same ideal: the harmonious and mature person who knows that he can survive only in a voluntarily acknowledged set of physical and metaphysical responsibilities. The more activist and character-building tendency of the gentleman concept, and the more contemplative tendency of the scholarly ideal (which, in the last analysis, came out of the medieval university) — in other words, *Humanitas* and *Veritas* complement each other like the two sides of a triangle. But the basis of the triangle must be *Religio,* for neither our moral nor our intellectual values can live on themselves. For their continual support and direction they need a faith or a metaphysics of devotion to a universal order reflecting itself in the best of our human endeavors.

6. *Some Words about the Specialist*

If American higher education loses contact with these great traditions, it will lose itself, because it has thriven on them historically and spiritually. Only with these traditions in the background can the American university venture into new experiments without being overwhelmed by the lure of attractive but hollow novelties and techniques.

Finally, only with these traditions can professional specialization continue without becoming a parasite that kills the tree on which it grows. The modern alarm over specialization is much more a sign of weakness of the institution in which it grows than a proof of its necessarily evil character. Specialization becomes evil only when severed from the totality of human interest.

After all, is not specialization, or, as we may also call it, "concentration," the concomitant to the mind's venture into more and more areas of culture and nature unknown to our ancestors? Do our students prefer the specialized courses only because they are narrow-minded, or because there they feel the closer connection between their studies and their calling and, consequently, a stronger motivation? Is there not much justified inspiration in a young person's hope that his specialty may help him to become a good physician, a good lawyer, a good teacher, or a good engineer, and thus a more useful member in his society?

The task is not, as some writers believe, to fight "the evil of specialization" in the holy name of the traditional *artes liberales*. As if a scholar who wants to write and teach well in any one field of the humanities were not himself bound to become a specialist! As a matter of fact, one can discover the worst specialists exactly among those men who constantly argue against their academic colleagues in the laboratories, or the state teachers colleges, or the graduate schools. We should never cease to criticize each other in a healthy spirit of understanding, but we have greater responsibilities than family quarrels. We must convince the teachers of any one academic subject that, though specialists by necessity, they have to enhance their effectiveness by a deepening consciousness of the total aspirations of the human mind. The human mind wants to know ever more and more, but most of all it wants to know for what end it knows and towards what goal it strives.

When one speaks about this problem with a certain type of scholar, one discerns a fear of "romanticism"; some scholars think that they are being asked to interrupt their work with occasional pious sermons about humanity, philosophy, or "even" religion. This suspicion proves the deterioration of scholarship we have run into. Irrespective of the problem, still undecided among the greatest scientists, of whether the universe of mind and nature is of merely mechanical or of teleological character, why should it not be possible to show not only the mechanism in the workings of nature, but also its dynamic and beauty? Why shouldn't the student in the laboratory, in addition to learning exact methods of research, also learn something about the logic of science and its implications with respect to a modern theory of knowledge? The problems of causality and chance, and of heredity and selection, stretch far beyond the departments of physics and biology. They are also general human problems which have stirred the minds of thinking men for centuries. Why should the student of law not be introduced into philosophical anthropology, ethics, and the history of the concept of justice in connection with his learning the tricks and rituals of the legal profession? May not such philosophical knowledge even be highly practical in a period of crisis and change such as ours? Should the engineer be interested only in machines, the architect only in building houses, and the physician only in sickness? Are not all these branches of applied thought also concerned with the profoundest revelations of nature and the most urgent problems of man and society? If dealing with them is heresy to the ideal of "exact scholarship," then exact scholarship becomes heresy to culture, and both will finally perish in the dilemma.

If professional, or specialist, education is understood as part of man's grand labor in the service of *Humanitas* and *Veritas*, then there is no reason why we should not welcome it. Realistically speaking, specialization is already the master in the house of higher education. The question cannot be how to drive this master out, but how to teach him to cooperate by telling him that his own welfare depends on the welfare of the whole.

7. *The Doctorate Frenzy and the Devaluation of Titles*[4]

There exists in mobile societies a general tendency to give to wider circles of the people privileges held previously only by a few. This tendency stems from both positive and negative trends in man. They are positive trends in that men of talent wish to participate in greater responsibility and knowledge, in that the "natural rights of man" assert themselves against monopolies and exploitation, and in that mature nations no longer want to be governed, but to govern themselves — whatever that may be. Negative are these trends in that they often spring from envy and resentment rather than from genuine desire for wider ranges of productivity. Thus the noble words of equality, liberty, and fraternity have been used throughout history by the great as well as by the greedy, by the inspired as well as by those for whom excellence is not a value to aim at, but an object of hatred.

Consequently we find in all developed societies two, so to speak, inverse lines of motion, either of which is characterized by good as well as by evil traits. We have an aggression against privilege which is good in so far as it expresses all that we cherish in the true idea of democracy, but evil in that it yields to covetousness and vulgarity. Against this leveling tendency men have always tried to establish and preserve distinctions, which is good in so far as it cultivates the sense of standard, but evil when it creates undeserved advantages of a minority, or defends prerogatives which have lost their original meaning.

All the good and evil sides in the battle between distinction and equality show also in the history of the academic

---

[4] See in this connection also Howard Mumford Jones, *Education and World Tragedy*, Harvard University Press, 1946.

world. Often, and rightly, this world has been blamed for
its remoteness from the life of the common man, but certainly, with respect to the strife of ambitions and the greed
for external honors the professors never hesitated to join
the *profanum vulgus*. The old universities were guilds and
were second to no other association in the general medieval
scramble for privileges, seals, plumage, and priority in pro-
cessions. As early as the thirteenth century they established
elaborate rituals and ceremonies about the conveyance of
honors and titles, generally connected with high forms of
conviviality and ending sometimes in bloody fights between
town and gown, the town presenting the sober, and the
gown the alcoholic element. We also find an amazing number of ordinances about the procedure of examinations
proving that even the *domini* and *doctores* in the big universities were not intransigent to the temptations of bribery
and nepotism.

On the other hand, we find in academic history definitely
equalitarian tendencies. In the sixteenth century the
Protestant radical Karlstadt for religious reasons advocated
the abolishment of degrees. He had read in St. Matthew
XXIII that we should call no man "Rabbi" or "Master," and
transferred this admonition to the academic level. The
French revolutionaries of 1789 thought that academic titles,
together with all other caste differences, should be done
away with for political reasons. Both examples, needless
to say, reveal a strong democratic tendency; both times,
however, it was soon discovered that without the earthly
motive of reward the *magistri* neglected their teaching and
the *studiosi* their learning.

Today, it seems, we solve the problem of Christian and
democratic equality by driving everybody through the doctorate mill who aspires at a position that has even the slight-

est semblance of scholarly creativeness: college teachers who never intend, and have not even a chance, to write a book or an essay; school superintendents and principals who hope for better income; psychologists who administer tests in clinics and psychopathic hospitals; and government officials who probably believe that American bureaucracy will be more attractive if executed in a truly scientific spirit. Needless to say, intellectual mass production and mass consumption lower the standard. Some so-called "research" on the doctorate level is repulsive to anyone who still has some sense of scholarship. Certain newly created doctorates no longer require a knowledge of foreign languages. It seemingly does not matter whether the bearer of the highest academic title is internationally illiterate or not. In other departments one accepts reports about some kind of project, or one believes that the candidate has lived up to scientific standards if he surrounds a perfectly obvious, or totally insignificant, topic with the halo of experimental or statistical procedure.

Of course, every university that goes one step farther in lowering the requirements for the doctorate examination talks about a "reform," while it should talk about a deterioration. And no doubt, someone in the committee on reform speaks also about the school's obligation to "the spirit of democracy."

But do we really help the cause of democracy by driving more and more people up to the level of the Ph.D. or Ed.D. or Sc.D., whatever the name may be, who need not be theoretically creative in order to discharge their professional duties honorably, and who could never become real scholars even if they so wished?

As a matter of fact, rather than doing democracy a favor, we do it harm. We force more and more people to prolong their studies, to incur heavy expenses and perhaps debts, to postpone a normal family life with children, all this for a purpose which is not really their own. For they would not submit to the whole procedure if it were not imposed upon them by the co-operation of appointing authorities and universities, the two working in the framework of a bureaucratized society which no longer puts its faith in personalities but wants to have the false security of stamps, certificates, and titles. To A. Lawrence Lowell, former president of Harvard, the following remark is ascribed: "Observing the continual prolongation of studies and, at the same time, the tendency to retire people at an increasingly earlier age, I wonder when the last examination and the first hint at retirement may coincide."

The imposition of sacrifice is generally justified if the labor involved is in a sound relation to the reward which both the individual and his society may receive. In a scholarly life one might even appreciate the intrinsic value inherent in serious research. But how can there be such compensation in certain doctorate studies so void of human value that they contribute nothing to a student's personal education except perhaps in terms of self-discipline and patience, virtues that could be learned also by devotion to a worth-while cause?

College teachers and administrators are today increasingly concerned with the problem of teaching on the college level. They are disturbed by the fact that so many instructors are unable to inspire their students. This lack of inspiration is partly due to the academic teachers' early specialization, to their exposure in college to inefficient professors whom they unconsciously imitate, to lack of comparative and comprehensive knowledge, and to a training in which the critical and analytical attitude prevents the development of vision and the courage of interesting interpretation of human situations. One sticks to "facts." But can facts be isolated from their historical setting? Can they, so far as human societies are concerned, be divorced from motives which can be understood only intuitively? And can their enumeration in lecture form interest a young intelligent student who knows that he can find them in any textbook?

What remedy, in all likelihood, will most of our college administrators propose for the improvement of college teaching? They will try to recruit their staffs with men who have the doctorate degree. For the sake of academic prestige they will force their younger instructors, who could use their vacations for some independent reading and thinking, to attend summer schools for gradually piling up the necessary number of course units; they will force them to subject themselves to preliminary and general examinations; and all this after these men and women have already gone through a bachelor's and master's trial, passed dozens of course examinations, written paper after paper, and enjoyed hundreds of tests and quizzes. Must we not marvel at the resisting power of the human soul which makes it possible that after all these inflictions there are still some young people left with imagination, initiative, and sympathy for their fellow creatures? And since the state teachers colleges will try to live up to the Joneses — in other words, the liberal arts colleges — they also will prefer instructors with doctorate degrees. Of course, they should have the best type of teachers. But is this high quality type represented by men and women who have written theses on an obscure phase of American history, on the family relations of a primitive tribe, on the psychology of rats, on school busses in the State of X, or on the payment of janitors? Thus, while we believe that we should do everything in our power to raise the standards of teaching, we direct the whole educational system into a barren form of intellectualism which has little to do with either good scholarship or good and popular education. Are the scientists, who generally have kept their doctorate work on a higher achievement level than the humanists, for this reason less effective in their role as researchers, engineers, architects, or teachers?

What would be the way out of the dilemma? In order to answer this question we have to make an excursion into the history of the American doctorate degree.

The American Ph.D. is largely taken over from the institution of the *Doctor philosophiae* of the German universities of the nineteenth century. These universities were built on a preparatory school, the Gymnasium, which fulfilled rather well its purpose of a general and liberal education and of imbuing the future university students with good working habits. A graduate from the old good Gymnasium, just as a graduate from a good French *lycée,* was scholastically at least as far advanced as an American college student after his sophomore year. Furthermore, not only before but also at the end of the university studies the governments of the more centralized countries on the European continent controlled scholastic achievements rather effectively. In Germany those who wanted to enter the career of law, of medicine, of teaching in the secondary schools, or of theology had to undergo a professional entrance examination in which both the university professors and a representative of the government, or, in the case of theology, a representative of the Landeskirche (the state church) was present. Within this kind of framework there was no need for the elaborate system of bachelor's or master's degrees. They ceased to exist, while the doctorate, for a considerable period of the nineteenth century, could be preserved as a definitely scholarly degree — except in the field of medicine where the title of doctor has a different history in almost all countries. In addition, Germany had for the prospective university teacher the so-called habilitation, or the *examen pro facultate docendi*. In other words, whereas Germany, in contrast to Anglo-Saxon countries, abolished the medieval institution of the *baccalaureus* and *magister*, it retained the medieval custom of a rigid and solemn entrance examination for the career of the academic teacher, consisting of an oral examination, a public lecture before the whole university, and a treatise which had to be a scholarly "contribution" of independent and high quality. The combination of the Gymnasium as a preparatory school, which allowed the student a high degree of freedom during his studies (without course examinations and similar requirements), and the doctorate as the first and the habilitation as the second examination for the candidate of the scholarly profession made possible a high degree of creativeness in the relatively small number of German universities.

Unfortunately, things changed when, since the end of the nineteenth century, the title of "doctor" lost more and more its definitely scholarly character and became a desirable ornament for more and more people in the professions. The more ambitious of the secondary school teachers wanted to have the *Dr. philosophiae*. It was also good for an appointment as a literary critic, an adviser of a publishing house, or a state theater; lawyers liked to put the *Dr. juris* on their shingles; and when such new disciplines as government, economics, business, or pedagogy appeared in the academic theater, new doctorate titles were created in addition to the old *Dr. philosophiae*. Also in the United States we have now a steadily expanding list of academic honors. And like the Germans we also degrade the scholarly significance of the doctorate degree by giving it to politicians, generals, business executives, donors, and other people who may merit public attention but certainly not for any scholarly contribution.

It came about, then, that in Germany in the period of unemployment before the days of Hitler, men and women who had to accept mediocre positions had made heavy sacrifices in time, money and labor in order to pass the doctorate examination. A person with some practical training could have filled the job just as well and even better, but many businessmen preferred to have a "Herr Doktor" among their clerks and salesmen. Perhaps he cost them even less than a man who had matured in practical life.

Are we going to take over the social evil of useless overschooling? During the great times of German scholarship young Americans crossed the ocean and brought with them a lot of good learning. No doubt, this cultural interchange and even the doctorate examinations helped to raise the standards of the American universities in the days of President Gilman of Johns Hopkins and President Eliot of Harvard. A considerable number of colleges changed from insignificant institutions to academic centers of international reputation. I am far from denying that in many cases today wisely administered doctorate examinations still raise the level of scholarship and research.

If one takes over some good peculiarities from another culture, however, must one also repeat its errors?

There are available other examples by means of which we could arrive at a wholesome comparative judgment. Let us look at the Scandinavian universities, which in spite of their small size and number today surprise the world every year by the quality and amount of their scholarly production. Or let us look at the old English universities. In contrast to

Germany and the United States, these universities have kept the doctorate degree on a high level. There is no danger that it will become a threat of useless delay to young people who feel fitted for responsible positions, or a badge for those who want to have a promotion or a better income regardless of whether or not they are interested in scholarship. Nor does there exist the menacing alliance between academic teachers, public administrators and other kinds of bureaucrats who make the nation believe that one cannot learn through participation in the practical tasks of life but must sit on school benches for one-third of a normal productive life.

Indeed, the universities of the United States have maneuvered themselves into a strange position. They have neither the advantages of the German secondary schools and universities of the nineteenth century with *Lernfreiheit* (freedom of learning) and *Lehrfreiheit* (freedom of teaching), nor do they have the good features of the English collegiate system. They have the disadvantages of both: from the more recent German development the exaggerated emphasis on the doctorate degree, and from the English collegiate system the rather restricting control of the student and the cumbersome system of the bachelor's and master's examinations.

We could even learn from the most recent post-war developments in Europe. It is not merely the result of "reactionary" tendencies on the part of the older intellectual groups of Europe that they try to prevent the destruction of the last remnants of classical education. Nor is it snobbishness that at the same time they fight for the restoration or the preservation of the truly scholarly character of the doctorate degree. They know that they have the choice either to regain a good general preparation on the secondary level, or to introduce "general education" courses, class examinations, and all kinds of intermediate degrees during the period of university studies. For this measure they have neither the inclination nor the money. The population of Europe is financially incapable of extending the professional preparation of the younger generation to the degree it is extended in the United States. From bitter experience they have learned that the least expensive preparation for the professions is high quality.

If in this country we want to have high professional standards and good teachers in our colleges, let only those be awarded the doctorate who, in addition to the title, really want and need an extended preparation for later scholarly work. If they need financial support, let us create sufficient stipends; for this is the duty of democracy. But let us in all departments raise the master's degree to a level which again gives the appointing agencies the confidence that its bearers are well equipped for superior work as teachers in high schools and colleges, or as government officials, school administrators, psychologists, guidance officers and holders of other positions which demand a certain degree of scholarly erudition, but do not require creative scholarship.

It is the tragedy in lowering the top level, in our case the doctorate degree, that the other degrees also fall in value. We already have the situation that the bachelor's degree of today is worth no more than the graduation certificate from high school was fifty years ago, that the master's degree has about the same value a bachelor's degree had to the fathers and grandfathers of our students. Therefore we have now all sorts of super-graduate schools and institutions for advanced study.

Educators have a public trust from the parents of the nation. If the parents discover that the education of their children becomes more and more prolonged, laden with degrees and examinations, and at the same time more and more unrewarding, they will lose respect for our higher schools. There are signs that such a state of unrest already exists.

Thus, rather than indulging in the temptations of social inertia with all its resulting cruelties, let at least our universities prove themselves worthy of their leading position in modern society. Let them examine not only their students, but first of all themselves and their whole system of teaching and examining.

8. What to Do?

We have now dealt with the past and present of our universities in order to discover the main factors which constitute a culturally productive form of higher education. In this attempt we found that it is the obligation of the university to combine, in one and the same process, education toward true humaneness and education toward a scholarly approach to the world of man and nature.

Since many of our remarks were critical with respect to our present achievements, the question may properly be asked: What to do about it?

The first and most important answer would be not to imitate the past, but to renew in oneself the spirit which, in certain periods, has made the universities symbols of moral and intellectual excellence. We cannot and should not think and write today like the great thinkers or poets of the past. However, we can see to it that the fountainheads of their inspiration do not get clogged and that we do not through poor procedures kill in the bud the strength of human creativeness. Anthropologists cannot detect any change in the nature of man since the dawn of civilization. Yet, in very deep dimensions of his existence he changes constantly between superficiality and depth, complacency and courage.

History is a cemetery of peoples who hoped to survive just because they existed, and it is an arch of triumph for peoples who were able to open the gates of the mind, to grasp a great purpose, and to pursue it faithfully and rationally.

Only if we make the subject matter we teach transparent toward the strivings, the failures, and the permanent sources of human creativeness, only then can the haphazard educational groping of today be replaced by directed action. With this deeper principle understood, there will be possible the combination of clarity concerning the universal goal with elastic adaptation to specific situations.

But, said Michelangelo, "Trifles make perfection, and perfection is no trifle." So we may also here be permitted to speak about seeming trifles, in order to pass from them on to more general issues.

1. Arrange the reading assignments of the students so that they have time to reflect on what they read. Bring about a mutual understanding among instructors with respect to their demands upon the student and recommend books which direct the mind not to masses of trivial material, but toward something worth while thinking about. Facts alone are not truth; they become truth only through the spirit in which they are interpreted.

Some universities now have courses in quick reading for slow readers. It might be advantageous to have also courses in slow reading for quick readers.

2. Arrange the written assignments of the students in such a way that they are not only part of an examining procedure, but a part of his learning and inner development. Certain examinations, given even at our best universities, truly deserve no other name but "quizzes" — "quiz" originally meaning "an absurd question, designed to puzzle or make ridiculous."

Instead of many short papers, we should ask for one which gives the student an opportunity to work thoroughly and with personal interest. Propose for each paper several topics, so that the students can relate their personal interests to their assignments.

3. Oral examinations should still remain a part of academic training, especially on the higher level. Much has been said against their subjectivity. This criticism is correct, though it also applies to written examinations. Even such mechanical devices as true-false tests provide no reliable criteria as to a student's quality. Unfortunately, many professors are unaware that good oral examining is an art. The examiner should first encourage the student and establish confidence, and then go deeper into a problem and its ramifications in order to find out what the student knows, what he does not know, whether he knows that he does not know, and whether he knows how to think, to find out, to discriminate, to inter-relate, and to express himself. Such an examination requires discipline among the members of the committee. They must not interrupt a sequence of ideas (for showing off and for hearing themselves talk) but wait until their time has come and then to continue the process of *search* and not merely the questioning.

4. Consider whether it might be good for freshmen to have introductory courses in methods of study. It is deplorable to see how much time students lose because they do not know how to find the right book, how to use it, how to discover the necessary bibliographical material, how to organize a somewhat complex subject. The professors in the various departments, the library, and the laboratories should work together in order to make such a course interesting and totally different from the appalling aridness characteristic of the typical books on "How to Study" or "How to Write

a Doctorate Thesis." Rather than be recommended, such books as well as the typical "Short Guides Toward . . ." should be forbidden. They are generally written by second-rate men who compensate for their lack of imagination and creativeness by specializing on mechanics. Such men fail also to see that every individual has a somewhat different method of approach, and that every topic has its distinctive methodical facet.

5. The principle of variety applies also to teaching: there is not one universally valid method. Certainly we have, partly as a consequence of large classes, too many lecture courses. We should have more seminars and free exchange of ideas. Even a typical lecture course should be followed or interrupted by discussion hours. On the other hand, there are professors who know how to inspire through their oratory, who give their students a sense of logical structure and architecture of thought, and who fill their lectures with much more content and personality than is possible if students have constantly to listen to each other's half-baked wisdom. Also, there can be more real "participation" in listening to one great man than in talking to many small ones.

6. An enormous amount of time could be saved for instructors and students, and much money for the administration, by eliminating courses which give nothing but information available in good handbooks. Do not believe that everything has to be taught which a student may meet later on in his profession. Academic learning is first of all a learning of the principles by which the mind of man tries to understand and master the world as far as he has access to it, even though, of course, these principles have to be taught in relation to subject matter and in relation to their correct and imaginative application. People who cannot profit from this kind of learning should not study.

7. Give time to the teacher. Committee work, if dealing with principal and important topics, is a part of mutual learning and acquaintance, but many committees are the result of bad habits, laziness and escape of responsibility. Professors should not be permitted to teach summer school year after year. The long vacations of the academic profession are, besides the necessary recreation, for serious and uninterrupted study, which is less and less possible during the regular term. College presidents who ask for "superior young instructors" and then impose upon them sixteen hours of weekly teaching force promising men down to the level of mediocrity.

8. In larger universities with few possibilities for community living the houses and dormitories should be centers of such life. If the central administration has no chance to do it, the masters of the houses should see to it that the students become actively interested in the affairs of the local community. It is undemocratic to send students out into life who from their sixth year on have been in private schools and other walled institutions without any real contact with the American people.

9. Graduate work should not be considered "technical" education in the sense that it becomes the end of "liberal" education. Such a distinction rests on the logically interesting confusion that of two inter-related activities either one can be inferior to the other: liberal education is thought to be a matter for neophytes and without practical value, and graduate education is thought to be for special professional practice and consequently without universal value. But the true specialist, while reaching deeper into a problem, reveals at the same time its relation to constantly widening aspects of knowledge and research. If we want to have men in the professions who combine expert skill with creative

talent we have to cultivate the liberal — i.e., the intuitive and imaginative — faculties just as much as the sense for, and skill in, details. Productive research depends on both.

10. The doctorate degree should be the reward for high forms of creative erudition and for nothing else.

11. The best way to ruin scholarship in a university is to invite streamlining efficiency experts. They bring disaster to all human activities which depend on freedom, love, sympathy, devotion, and the grace of creativeness.

The history of higher learning as well as the history of the fine arts proves clearly that seeming waste is the condition of highest productivity.

> The more the marble wastes,
> The more the statue grows.
> (*Michelangelo*)

12. The Harvard Report on *General Education in a Free Society* (page 104) says rightly: "There is no educational reform so important as the improvement of teaching." It says so with respect to secondary schools, but this statement is just as true at the college level. What can be done about it? Nothing would be more doomed to failure than a forcing of college instructors into typical courses on methods of teaching. Some promise may lie, however, in the arrangement of discussion groups within the individual departments where the best teachers in the field could exchange ideas and experiences with young instructors. To such discussions a man with systematic interests in education could be invited in order to relate the specific to the general findings of educational psychology and philosophy.

13. There is certainly a relation between quantity and quality. Too small a university can no longer offer what students of today need to learn, but too big a university

tends to become an educational factory. An institution of higher learning should expand according to the inner development of unfolding scholarship and the availability of men of quality, rather than with the desire for external size. If this principle is followed, an institution will be sound and there will be no lack of students.

14. There are, of course, prerequisites for the fulfillment of the cultural mission of the university which go far beyond its own orbit into the relationship of higher learning with the totality of culture. I have dealt with this topic in a paper prepared for the ninth meeting of the Conference on Science, Philosophy and Religion with the title: "On the Rise and Decline of Higher Education"[5] and may be permitted to enumerate here briefly what I called the conditions requisite to a healthy state of higher education.

a. The universities must satisfy the intellectual and professional ambitions of a period; in other words, fulfill the function of intellectual leadership.

b. They must be helpful in the development of methods of thinking and research.

c. They must live under a system of patronage sympathetic to the idea of *libertas philosophandi*.

d. The university must be the symbol of the universality of knowledge.

e. It must be the symbol of the continuity of culture.

f. It must fulfill the function of *Sinndeutung*, or philosophical interpretation of the civilization in which it operates.

The last three points could also be phrased in form of the following questions:

Will it be possible to relate the ever-expanding sphere of

---

[5] See *Goals for American Education*, Ninth Symposium of the Conference on Science, Philosophy and Religion, edited by Bryson, Finkelstein, and MacIver, New York, Harper and Brothers, 1950, pp. 1-18.

descriptive-experimental knowledge and research to a deeper dimension of thought from which, first, all our mental endeavor receives an inner unity in spite of its manifoldness; which, second, allows us to link new ideas to the great chain of thought and thus gives us that feeling of historical continuity without which change becomes chaos; and which, third, gives us assurance that humanity and its endeavors are not just a whim of an inscrutable creator but a meaningful part of a meaningful whole?

If those responsible for our colleges and universities will have these conditions in mind, not as something that could ever be fulfilled, but as a goal to be striven for, then the details of administrative and curricular organization will order themselves according to the particular social and cultural conditions. It then makes no difference whether or not one has a special department for "liberal" or for "general" education; or whether one puts these responsibilities at the beginning or at the end of a student's career. For all these special devices of the last decade are but indications that modern higher education has given up the claim to accomplish the integration of humaneness and scholarship through the totality of its operations. The two sides, liberal and/or general education, and specific education, have fallen apart. They can be brought together only through teachers who themselves, whatever they teach, represent to their students the living synthesis of *Veritas* and *Humanitas*.

So we return at the end of this practical discussion to the philosophical-ethical foundations of higher learning. If these foundations crumble, our universities will degenerate into training schools. If they become strong again, the universities will be the bulwarks to protect the best in our Western civilization.

CHAPTER SEVEN

Adult Education

1. *Mutual Education in Daily Life*

Ralph Waldo Emerson says in his essay on "Education":

It is ominous, a presumption of crime, that this word Education has so cold, so hopeless a sound. A treatise on education, a convention for education, a lecture, a system, affects us with slight paralysis and a certain yawning of the jaws. . . . Education should be as broad as man.[1]

But education — unless it is as broad as man — has not only a cold and hopeless sound; it can also have a petty and offensive sound. Something rebels in us when we feel the "schoolmaster" encroaching upon our liberty and telling us what we ought to do and to think, though he himself may have less experience than other people.

Youth also, and often the best among them, feel this antagonism; they sense a hidden enemy in a certain type of teacher, as if he were chosen by destiny to lead them away from their own path with all its adventures and all its errors. There are things in life which are too great and serious, even for the young, to be disposed of by a teacher shaking his finger.

For these reasons the term "adult education" is unfortunate. Certainly, an adult ought always to learn; he ought

---

[1] *Works*, Century Edition, Boston, Houghton Mifflin Company, Vol. X, p. 133.

never to slacken in his willingness to educate himself and to be educated. But we all wish this education to be the flower and the fruit of our own growth, and not just the product of outside influence.

What is true of adult individuals is also true of peoples as a whole. Nations cannot be "educated" or "re-educated" from outside. Some may be "backward"; others may have committed terrible crimes against the spirit of humanity. All have. Yet in backwardness there may be more dignity and genuineness than in a certain type of progress; and the tragedy and complexity inherent in collective guilt are much too profound for "educators" who have spent their lives only in classrooms and libraries.

As we have already sufficiently indicated, the school-masterly climate in a nation only enhances the trend toward waiting for directions from outside, toward passivity and negative forms of collectivism. Is not a liberal and progressive man of today sometimes tempted to wish he had lived in the nineteenth century, in spite of all its obvious defects? There was at least dynamic and drive — even the suppressed classes and nations created their progressive ideologies and utopias — whereas now we live ideologically on an economy of scarcity: and this exactly at a time when democracy's responsibility for itself and the world is greatest.

Even our private life does not really profit from its being relieved of thousands of activities necessary before the era of ready-made clothes and food, of the laundry man and the vacuum cleaner. There was certainly no cultural value in all the drudgery of the housewife who had to fetch water from the well, make the fire, milk the cow, weave the linen, and bear a dozen children. These women died early, and they were old and exhausted when many of our women are still on the crest of their vigor and beauty. But what vigor and beauty is there in the life of a woman who lives in a small city apartment, goes out shopping, turns on the radio when she comes home if she wants to hear a voice, and has to wait for children until it is dangerous or impossible to have any? Or, if she has only one, she has to send him at the age of three to nursery school because otherwise he would have no playmates, little exercise, and little fresh air. And how many men who work from nine to five o'clock in a store, factory, or office are secretly longing for a life of independence and initiative? Yet they bear the boredom because they and their families need security. And in the course of time they become egotistic.

The carelessness of many married people for their fellow men is amazing. They choose to bore each other rather than to invite young men and women who spend their time in dormitories, restaurants, and drugstores. The loneliness of unmarried women, especially those who go from college into professional life, is sometimes so dreadful that they prefer a marriage without love, or the silliest cocktail parties with disappointing affairs, to the life in their single rooms. With only a small amount of neighborly initiative we could provide for unmarried persons a home to meet not only adult men and women, but also children whom they would enjoy and who could enjoy them.

The best in the experience of the older generation, that which is too intangible to be communicated by books, is lost for the younger people because there is little chance for friendly conversations. How many privileged men in our so-called classless society have ever thought of seeking contact with workers in their neighborhood, not for reasons of charity, but for an exchange of ideas among groups which live in one and the same community with such divergent interests and chances? What would it do to the life of a nation if each of us tried to demechanize it through his own personal effort?

This would be the basic premise of adult education.

2. *Our Present Adult Education*

Unfortunately, by far the greatest part of our formal and institutionalized adult education is not of such a kind that it could help people to understand how to live a fully human and humane life. Whereas with respect to secondary and tertiary education we had to complain that it was too verbal and intellectual, the only form of adult education that is really flowering in this country is vocational.

This statement should not be understood in any derogatory sense. People with drive feel that with a better specialized training in bookkeeping or a craft they can acquire a better position, so they gladly use any opportunity that offers itself. Men and women, after a full and strenuous work day or in periods of worrying and unemployment attend evening classes from simple arithmetic and English grammar up to specialized accounting.

In comparison to this useful and technical adult education, the typical cultural courses in Community Centers and similar institutions are unsatisfactory. Surely, there should be lecture clubs, town hall meetings over the radio, university extension courses of non-vocational character, forums, and whatever contributes to more knowledge. But there are people who read so many books and listen to so many lectures that they become increasingly more confused. And each of us can ask how many of the single lectures he has heard have really had a molding influence in his life. Only those lectures make a lasting impression which have touched us emotionally. Not the information, but the excitement lives on in us.

The typical community centers seem to be afraid of intellectual excitement, however, because they are afraid of "controversial issues." They prefer lecture courses or seminars on the history of philosophy, of art, and religion, or courses on painting and sculpturing, to courses which touch the vital problems of the intelligent truth-seeker and socially or politically interested citizen. Schools for adults which have the courage to enter the areas of conflict are under suspicion and have been forced to close their doors.

During the past decade the workers' unions have set up their own education programs. These are helpful. The work done by the International Ladies' Garment Workers Union is excellent. Generally, however, there is a lack of good instructors, and naturally many of these programs are intended to serve the training of local union officers. In a way, then, they also are vocational.

3. Adult Education and the Ideal High School

There could be a decisive stimulation for a new adult education if it were carried on in connection with our ideal high school, its buildings, and its campus. We have already spoken of this great opportunity to connect the school with the interests of the adults. The new school's Community House could be the center for all kinds of recreating leisure. In the halls and workshops men of practical life could assemble in the evening in order to discuss, under systematic leadership, the constantly advancing techniques applied in our commercial and industrial life. Others may like to use the libraries, and still others may arrange classes on philosophical and social problems in which the teachers of the humanities could be useful and, in addition, learn much themselves. It is one of the great handicaps in the development of the average teacher that he has mostly to do with younger people who have to listen and cannot correct him. If the high school and adult education were co-operating, the school might be lifted out of this isolation. A mutual enrichment might develop between teachers and laymen, quite different from the typical relation between the school teacher and the school board of today.

The Community House and the whole school campus could also be the place for the emotional elevation of the adult, which in our times is so badly neglected. Why should not parents and children, as they already do in some progressive schools, co-operate in the preparation and performance of a play, a concert, or a pageant? There are hundreds of thousands of children who walk from a dreary family life and gloomy living quarters to a drab school building and then come home again, until the young vigor releases itself in the adventures of a gang which bring an otherwise normal youngster into the courts. How much would it help to bring young and old together if our society spent only a small part of its imagination and energy by placing a new type of school in the center of the community's social life? When at the beginning of the fifteenth century the Italian humanist Vittorino da Feltre founded a school where the children were happy and the parents proud to participate, the good people of Mantua, so far accustomed to medieval scholastic coercion, called the new institution the *casa giocosa*, the house of cheerfulness.

Could we not, with our modern means, try again to have a *casa giocosa* in every community?

If these dreams came true, then one could perhaps build some of the People's Colleges in the neighborhood of the future high schools. For we need institutions where people, on leave of absence from their daily occupation, could stay for a period of about three to six months and enjoy all the advantages which Scandinavian young men and women derive from their Folk-High Schools, not only to their own personal profit, but to the profit of their communities and their nations.

This, of course, presupposes that the public school does not stuff its pupils with "education" in a period when they are longing for practical experience. As Bishop Grundtvig, the founder of the Danish Folk-High School, well knew, artificially prolonged formal education not only defeats its own purposes but also kills the desire for later mental development. The Scandinavian farmer who generally left school at the age of fourteen and worked on the field appreciated the chance to attend a Folk-High School when he reached seventeen or so, an age when many American boys, as an effect of false schooling, are "fed up."

4. Adult Education and the Great Issues of Life

Even the best possible development of all that we now usually understand by the term "adult education" would fall short of the ideal, however. While every movement in adult education which had some lasting influence on the life of the people, as for example the American Lyceum at the time of Horace Mann, might have *used* lectures, meetings, schools, and artistic performances, it was always much more than that. It included men and women who were concerned with a great issue of mankind.

When we speak of this wider concept of adult education, we will refer to three areas in particular: first, to adult education in relation to the social and political life of a nation; second, to adult education in relation to religious life; third, to adult education in relation to a uniting world view of secular character.

(a) *Social and Political Problems.* We speak first of adult education in relation to social and political life. When Benjamin Franklin in the year 1728 started the Junto, he wished to have "a club of mutual improvement . . . to be conducted in the sincere spirit of inquiry after truth, without fondness for dispute, or desire of victory." And out of the activities of the club sprang such practical effects as a fire department and a police department for the city of Philadelphia, subscription libraries, and increased paper currency.

When Bishop Grundtvig started the Danish Folk-High School movement, he wished to help the impoverished peasantry of his defeated country materially and spiritually. At the same time his educational reform plans issued from the broad and profound concept of life that he had found in the Christian tradition and in the daily reality of the hardworking Danish farmer.

When Bishop John H. Vincent, in the roughest period of American industrial expansion, had to defend the Chautauqua movement against the two great enemies of progress, aggressive reaction and social timidity, he could write the following words:

It is charged against this movement in behalf of popular education, that by it we shall unfit people in the humbler walks of life for the work we need from them. What shall we do for servants? What shall the dear girls of our homes do for subordinates to follow their bidding? And how, if people acquire taste, and begin to aspire after personal refinement, and to respect themselves, shall we be able to keep them in their places? What unendurable airs they will put on! And how we shall be at the mercy of our inferiors! . . .

I hope that we shall educate the people until the cultivated poor shall have more power than the ignorant rich; until the votes of the humblest cannot be bought by the bribes of the highest; until a man's right as a citizen, though he be poor as poverty, shall command all the resources of the nation in his defense and his protection; until the gates of the nation shall fly open on the sides of the east and of the west to welcome strangers from afar; until the comers-in at the east shall not dare to close the gates against the comers-in at the west; until parties and their leaders that discriminate between foreign classes, and cater to low race prejudices, shall be punished unto purification, or, if necessary, annihilated.

I hope that we shall train people to understand that manual labor is a degradation when brain-power and taste and heart are all sacrificed at the shrine of toil and bread and money. . . .

It is the mission of the true reformer, the true patriot, the true Christian, to offer Knowledge and Liberty and Refinement, Science, Literature, Art, and Religious Life, to all the people — everywhere.[2]

The moment we interpret the work of men such as Franklin, Grundtvig, and Vincent, it becomes evident that all good adult education hinges on an important premise. This premise rests on the possibility of connecting adult education with practical social goals. These goals will represent the interests of a specific group, but they must not be of a narrow partisan character: they must also include the interests of humanity as a whole.

With this statement we have emphasized a truth which applies not only to adult education but to all real education. It must be expressive of the will of the group in which it is carried on and by which it is supported, but it must also incorporate the general interests of humanity if it is to escape the perils of narrowness and final atrophy. In other words, education, though dependent on its more or less immediate social environment, must at the same time be anchored in the great universe of human values.

Is this not true of any other important movement in the history of mankind? Can a political party — which for good or evil, is also a sort of adult education — long survive if the people discover that it is but an instrument in the hands of a

---

[2] John Heyl Vincent, *The Chautauqua Movement*, Boston, Chautauqua Press, 1886, pp. 226 ff.

pressure group? Can a religious cult keep alive in a climate
of narrow sectarianism? Can even a whole nation long survive if it has become enslaved by its own isolated interests?

Here is the great dilemma in adult education and the reason why so many well-intended endeavors in this field are
so ineffective: how can one create movements which combine in themselves the qualities of both practicality and
human comprehensiveness? For the practical tends to be
narrow, and the comprehensive easily becomes general to the
degree of vagueness. No civilization, nor any form of education, however, can survive unless it shows its adherents
practical goals which carry at the same time the inspiration
of a great embrace.

There are many who despair, especially since the end of
the Second World War when again there are visibly piled up
before us almost insoluble physical and spiritual problems.

Fortunately, in the field of adult education we are not
without examples which may give hope. The Campbell
Folk School in Brasstown, North Carolina, founded by Mrs.
John C. Campbell, has become a center for the improvement
of adult living in one of the poorer districts of North Carolina. Following the pattern of the Danish Folk-High Schools,
the Campbell School invites young men and women to spend
several months there in order to learn better agricultural
methods, woodworking, and home industries such as weaving and carving, while they share in discussions about the
area, its history, problems and possibilities, and national and
international questions. Evenings are spent in folk dancing,
singing, and in general, activities of a lighter sort. If one
compares the homes of the farmers who have gone through
this school with those of their parents or their less fortunate
neighbors, one recognizes the difference immediately: better
houses and barns, the stock and fields in better condition,

good pictures on the walls and good books on a small but cherished shelf; happier parents and healthier children.

Many people have visited the Campbell School; yet, instead of several hundred, there are still few adult schools of this kind in this big country which has so much money and still so many backward districts. And even these schools are fighting for their existence.

There is the St. Francis Xavier University Extension movement which started from the town of Antigonish in Nova Scotia. Under the leadership of Father Tompkins it has helped a downtrodden population of fishermen, miners, and farmers to free themselves from the exploitation or, should we better say, the inefficiency of finance-capitalism. These men met after their long work hours, studied the methods of economic co-operation, founded credit unions, co-operative stores, small factories, sawmills, and gave an example to the whole province of what co-operative initiative of the common man is able to achieve, both economically and educationally. The movement is fascinatingly described by Bertram B. Fowler in his book, *The Lord Helps Those . . . How the People of Nova Scotia Are Solving Their Problems Through Cooperation.*[3]

This book ought to be widely read in every country, and not only by adults, but also by older pupils in their social studies. It probably contains more inspiration for truly democratic action than all the theoretical textbooks on government together.

Nor should we hesitate to mention in this context all those professional, political, industrial, and workers' associations which give their members a feeling of co-operation not only with respect to their particular interests, but of co-operation within a broader national or international scope. No doubt,

---

[3] New York, Vanguard Press, 1938.

many of these associations are nothing but devices for the safeguard of gains and profits. Though they have grown mammoth-like, they have remained provincial in mentality. The protection of interest through association, however, is almost as old as human civilization; both good and evil have been done in its name. The test as to whether, beyond the natural concern for security and expansion, a corporate body has an educational value lies in its capacity to widen the horizon of its members into problems of common welfare, and to interest them not only in more profit, but also in sacrifice for the common cause. The early workers' movement is an example of this kind; so is the battle of the German elementary school teachers for the improvement of the public schools in the middle of the nineteenth century. And in this country the recent struggle of the American Federation of Teachers has given its members a feeling of standing for a cause beyond a mere rise of salary.

It is one of the saddest features of our society that we know how, that we have examples of great political workmanship, and yet there is constant opposition to any new enterprise of public character.

There was and is opposition to the Tennessee Valley Authority, which has proved to be one of the most profitable enterprises in terms of increased industrial and agricultural production. To cite only one of the many items which could be quoted from David E. Lilienthal's book, *TVA, Democracy on the March:*[4]

Out of the thousands of reports in the records of the state agricultural institutions here is one from a Tennessee county, a land of "thin soil" and struggling people. In 1939 the TVA cooperative demonstration program began; in 1942 the annual report stated:

[4] New York, Harper and Brothers, 1944, p. 27.

"The number of milk cows increased 70%, from 43 head in January 1939 to 73 in the fall of 1942. . . . The number of beef cattle and veal calves marketed annually from the community has doubled during the last three years. . . . In addition, there has been a substantial increase in poultry and hog production for home use."

In five years one community in Virginia reports food production doubled.

But the TVA has been not only a release of natural energies; it has also been one of the most successful experiments in the release of human resources, a proof that governmental planning can be combined with the building of "regional pillars of decentralization."[5] In other words, the TVA has become one of the greatest ventures in adult education. Unless we find such combinations between collective and state-supported action on the one hand, and private initiative on the other hand, the great tradition of a free society will die out. We will have a society controlled either by big capitalist monopolies or by governmental bureaucracy, and the surrender of more and more individual enterprises and responsibilities to remote agencies of control will eventuate in the complete erosion of democracy.

When studying the great possibilities of moral and physical reconstruction applicable all over the world one can only be appalled at the crudeness of the methods that still dominate our international political life: "engineering" of human affairs which cannot be "engineered," displacements of millions of decent people which generally initiate the self-destruction of the displacing governments themselves — not only under the Nazis, but also under the auspices of "democracy" — de-industrialization rather than rechanneling of productive power, dividing countries rather than uniting continents, all this at a time when statesmen could read a

---

[5] *Ibid.*, p. 153.

document of such profound wisdom as David Lilienthal's description of the TVA. For there he speaks not only of an individual American enterprise, but also of the long-known relationship between physical pressure on the one hand and armed aggression on the other. Only "methods of unified development to create sustained productivity" can help in the great task of reconstruction.

The TVA has come to be thought of (here and abroad) as a symbol of man's capacity to create and to build not only for war and death but for peace and life. This is of great importance in the post-war period. For despair and cynicism in our own ranks will be a deadly enemy after Germany and Japan surrender. The immediate task of fighting keeps us tense. Once that tension is relaxed we must be prepared for a let-down, a bitter loss of faith and hope. When that time comes it will be desperately important as a matter of mental antisepsis that there be, in this country and abroad, many living proofs, of which the TVA is one, of the creative powers of mankind and of democracy's demonstrated and practical concern for the every-day aspirations of people.[6]

Our scientists know of the enormous resources of power contained in our earth and its rivers. But though day by day we could read, and still can read, about misery and unrest all over the world, how much has been done to encourage planned self-help on a really scientific basis? The diplomats would say that connecting loans with the imposition of co-operative self-help would violate the sovereignty of independent countries. Would the *people* really mind or just the governments and the power groups which rule them?

But in the course of time the American taxpayer may express his disinclination to pay and pay for keeping parts of the world in a state of artificial respiration, and the young men of this country may become tired of spending years of their life in occupation armies surrounded by an atmosphere of suspicion.

---

[6] *Ibid.*, pp. 205 ff.

Furthermore, which country is today really "sovereign" and "independent"?

Are not all farsighted people united in the belief that the old legal concept of sovereignty has been a plague rather than a blessing to mankind? Is it not our great historical opportunity to take now one step further in the liberation of humanity from moribund traditions and to lay the economic foundation for the future political unification of nations? The UN already has a splendid record in preventing disas- ters; let us hope the time has come for it to pass over from primarily preventive to comprehensive strategy.

The youth of Europe, once freed from false guides, would much prefer to use the shovel and build bridges and dams, than to live in the purgatory of aimlessness and the conflicts of nationalisms.

There are certainly courageous young people all over the world — American, English, French, Russian, German, Japan- ese — who would like to join together, give life to devas- tated areas, build up the destroyed cities, work with the people, and thus restore not only fields and dwellings, but also the broken morale of the world. These youths would wish to engage in such activities not just for the sake of other people and peoples, but for their own sake. For even in the victorious nations the danger of disillusion is near; it cannot be avoided by propaganda for the new internationalism through conferences, art exhibits, and musical entertain- ments symbolizing the "spiritual unity of humankind," but only by setting up uniting purposes and pursuing them through heroic action. So far the Quakers and some other small groups have set the first example of international work camps. Encouraging though this is, it is entirely insufficient.

Youth which has gone through the great experience of international co-operation may also envisage a new kind of international civilian service, or an "army" trained not for destruction, but for the amelioration of uncultivated districts, first in their own country, and then in other welcoming parts of this earth. Would it not be time now to materialize on a grand scale William James's ideas expressed in his famous essay the "Moral Equivalent of War"? The future "International Army" cannot suddenly be produced like a rabbit out of a hat; the beginning can be made only step by step. If the inevitable initial risks involved in the preparation of minds are not taken, we will never create the spirit which could prevent the future international armed force from becoming a newfangled power instrument in the hands of a big few who, in addition, will distrust each other, be distrusted by the smaller nations, and have their private armies besides.

Of course, here again we are talking about "utopias."

But is not the utopia sometimes more realistic than the inactivity of the so-called realist?

We know that the material and cultural decay of the European continent and of large parts of Asia would of necessity involve the plight of England and the isolation of the United States. We also know that the provision of minimum standards of living, if not assured in accordance with democratic principles, might finally be done by dictatorial collectivism. We ought to have learned by now that the urge for survival is stronger than the respect for systems of governments even if they are based on the proclamation of man's natural rights. In the state of misery and hopelessness man loses the sense for the dignity of the individual.

The educational influence of movements which unite the economic and cultural interests of man could also help bring about a rejuvenation of the inner political life in the Western

countries. The party system on which democracy and con-
stitutional government were built in the times of emerging
liberalism is one of the greatest powers in national and
international life; it is one of the most effective instruments
in adult education or adult miseducation. But in spite of
all this influence, it is only partly expressive of the real
needs and desires of the people. The ideologies and practices
of the great parties, in this and in other countries, are partly
residues from bygone times, and partly products of expedi-
ency. They pall on exactly those of our young men and
women who ought to be genuinely interested in politics, and
whose co-operation is needed. Today only uninformed
people are ignorant of the doubtful forces which often determine the choice of candidates and the character of political propaganda. Cynicism about politics is growing.

Partly cause and partly result of this negative development
is the increasing separation of party politics and govermental
bureaucracy from the personal interests and relations of the
people. Many of us no longer know for whom we vote, and
none of us can predict what hidden powers in the present
and future may force our delegates to decide one way or
another about national and international issues. Delegates
are anyhow more like party appointees than free representatives of the public will; even for the highest executives re-
election may play a greater role in their thinking than the
welfare of the people. Hence the growing feelings of helplessness or indifference which in several countries have
already caused the misled populace to try totalitarian systems, though each of these experiments has shown that
parliamentarianism, despite its obvious defects, is still the
best system to safeguard human rights. For governments
without public control become tyrannical.

Our form of government cannot thrive, however, only on

the meager consciousness that other forms of government
are still worse; it must root in a richer soil than that of
merely negative comparison. In order to avoid the dangers
of machinery and mechanization, modern complicated society needs all the vital cells of communal life which in
earlier times were provided by the guild, the community,
and the various voluntary brotherhoods. Certainly, we
ought not to try to bind new vines to old props; each period
of institutional life needs its special holds and braces. Yet
the truth remains that only co-operation, starting from the
bottom upwards and meeting response at the top, can serve
as a countercheck to soulless absolutism, whether it come
from exploiting minorities or from the power urge of the
masses.

Here lies the importance of the Co-operative Movement
as a potential in modern adult education. In countries where
it is strong, as in England and Scandinavia, many are already
convinced that it works as a fertilizing agent in the political
life of the nation. In contrast to the strife of parties and
politicians who live on this strife, the Co-operative Movement proves that it can rescue community life from decay,
that it can control prices the moment it has more than about
20 per cent of the production of an article in its hand, and
that it can improve the living conditions of the workers
without hurting the interests of the consumer.

G. D. H. Cole writes in his book, *A Century of Co-
operation:*[7]

Cooperation is a world-wide movement. It exists, in some
form, in every continent and in nearly every considerable country,
except where it has been temporarily crushed out by Fascist
oppression. . . . According to the statistics compiled by the International Labor Office there were in 1937 . . . no fewer than

7 The Cooperative Union, Ltd., Manchester, 1945, pp. 353 ff.

810,512 Cooperative Societies known to exist, with 143,260,953 members scattered over almost every part of the world.

And there can be no doubt that countries like Germany, China, and India either will build their economic future on principles similar to those of the Co-operative Movement, or they will be swayed from one political extreme to the other.

What — one may ask — has all this to do with adult education? The answer is that children as well as adults are educated not by discussing endless possibilities of choice, but by a directive environment. With the child it is the family and the little community around it; with the adult it is all this too, but at the same time it is the whole human society. Through the adult, this over-arching potency works even upon the schools and the children. How can there be steady human development if hundreds of thousands of families do not know whether or not their existence — perhaps for the second or third time — may be destroyed by clashes between nations? How can adults join in educational enterprises if, instead of clear goals, they have nothing before them but problems and problems, controversial issues, and a big question mark behind every public statement?

We return here to an insight already discussed in connection with secondary education: both freedom and learning are possible only before a plurality of choices, but this plurality must reside within an embracing order. However dimly conceived because of its evolving nature, unless an embracing order works somehow in the grounds of our existence, the strife ends in fatigue and the plurality of choices ends in chaos.

(b) *Adult Education and Religion.* Our emphasis on practical elements in adult culture does not negate the decisive importance of spiritual powers in humankind; on the contrary, one is not possible without the other.

In our Western civilization religion has always claimed to be the ultimate source and goal of education of both the young and adults, and to provide the daily life of man with universal aspirations. It is difficult to judge the degree to which this claim has been materialized, because mere external factors such as church membership do not indicate a person's actual participation in the religious tradition. In addition, for centuries the controversy has been going on as to what degree organized religion is a promoter of, or an obstacle to, the development of a free and humane civilization. Some great men, such as Auguste Comte, have expressed one belief in one period of their lives and the contrary in another, according to their changing criteria of evaluation.

From a sociologically descriptive point of view the picture seems to be this:

In England, and to a degree in the United States, liberal and socialist ideas as well as progressive politics have never developed such a hostile attitude toward the ecclesiastical tradition as has been the case in the Continental countries. The reason is that in the Anglo-Saxon countries the rationalist movement of the eighteenth century managed somehow to avoid the open split with the Judeo-Christian tradition; the attitude of Common Sense, as represented by John Locke in England and Benjamin Franklin in America, preferred logical inconsistency to jeopardizing the supposed moral and religious security of the people by philosophical radicalism. Furthermore, the decentralization of cultural and political life allowed for the continual creation of new sects which gave to suppressed groups a feeling of belonging and a chance for discussing their hopes and ideas. Thus frustration and its companion, uncritical aggressiveness, were more successfully avoided than in France, Spain, Russia, Italy, and Germany.

But avoiding an issue is rarely a solution. If the issue is deeply rooted in human nature it runs with them who want to run away; when they think it is buried, it suddenly pops up.

In the United States the compromising conventionalism of earlier times, the separation of church and state, and the growth of pragmatic philosophies have brought about an amazing degree of indifference about religious matters, especially in Protestant circles. This now begins to bother even those who are not genuinely interested in organized religion. They feel that forces may profit from this indifference which they like even less than the institutional churches: cynicism about social values and family life, juvenile delinquency, gangsterism, and the Communist threat to the social order of democracy. On the other hand the Catholic Church in the United States has developed more and more the well-known qualities of an *ecclesia militans*. They show especially in the struggle between the public and the denominational school systems and the political influence of Catholicism. Unfortunately, minority resentments enter into the picture and work both ways, from the top down and the bottom up.

In the Latin countries, perhaps excepting Spain, Catholicism among the majority of the educated people seems to be more a matter of custom and fear of an incalculable social void than of profound conviction; just as in certain Protestant circles one remains in the faith of the fathers much less because of a deeply felt urge than because of fear that "everything may break down" if the churches are deserted.

To what extent Christianity is a cultural factor in the great mystery of the modern world, Russia, is difficult to judge. The Orthodox Church is now apparently tolerated, and priests may have had some influence in the fighting army. But has the Orthodox Church perhaps met the new Russia on a plane which has little universal value from the Christian point of view? Those who know Dostoevski need no further information about the tendency in Russian Christianity to identify the past and future of "Holy Russia" with the will of God. Thus, it may not be too difficult to arrive at some sort of compromise between the religious past and the new government, which in addition to its missionary passion, displays more and more nationalist characteristics. But whatever it may be, certainly the meeting between Communism and the Orthodox Church will require a lot of rethinking on both sides, unless the Russian priests are happy to be just tolerated. The official party ideology, so far as we can see, has not yet made any concessions.

In the countries of Central Europe the Christian churches seem to have recovered some of their fading strength. They provided transcendental hope in years of tyranny, suppression, and destruction. To be sure, there have not been more martyrs among priests and ministers than among men and women inspired by social and political ideals. However, for a longer time than parties with definite political programs the churches could avoid the arena of political fight and refer to their supernatural and spiritual mission. When finally even they had to take a stand against the aggression of governments, they could, at least, not so easily be dissolved as the parties of the opposition.

Generally modern man, even if interested in religion, is no longer interested in theology. The varieties in the interpretation of the Holy Trinity or the Eucharist or the Laws no longer excite him to wage war on his neighbor. Whatever he may think about the relation of soul and body, he refuses increasingly to accept the promise of Heaven as a substitute for a normal measure of earthly happiness. With growing experience he becomes, so to speak, less and less dualistic; he wants to see earthly life and practice intertwined rather than separated.

Essentially, the interconnection between faith and social action has always been recognized by Christianity. Therefore the churches have expressed their ideas about liberalism and socialism, naturalism and supernaturalism, war and peace. But in the acute crises during the past centuries, nationalism has always triumphed over the universal claim of the Spirit. In addition, the churches have mostly taken a conservative, even a reactionary, point of view. But things begin to change. There is more social idealism in certain divinity schools than in any other university department.

Though sometimes high ecclesiastics alienate people with good taste by their difficulty in differentiating spiritual leadership from propaganda and Christian teaching from advertising, the fact remains that at present people listen to Christian leaders probably more than they did thirty years ago.

This now creates new and fateful responsibilities before the whole world.

Twice in its history the Christian Church has been confronted with great decisions which determined the future of civilization. Twice it failed: the first time in the Middle Ages when it arrogated to itself the spiritual and earthly power all in one, forced the governments to burn heretics, and meddled in the internal affairs of individual countries; the second time in the seventeenth century when it attempted to fetter the intellectual freedom of the scientists. While engaging in the first venture, the Church was unaware of the determination which lay in man's desire for national and individual independence. Thus it helped bring about exactly what it tried to avoid, a rebellion of protesting sects and the final split of the Western Church. In the seventeenth century and later, the Church arrogated to itself the role of the arbiter in matters of science. It failed to recognize the power in man's intellectual curiosity and search for empirical truth. Thus it caused the rift between the religious and the scientific consciousness of modern man. Yet, in both cases it imagined that it defended a sacred against a sinful principle: in the first case the unity of Christendom and the apostolic tradition, in the second case the philosophical unity of Aristotelianism and the Biblical revelation.

Today religion is inevitably involved in the struggle of the Western nations against Communism. The situation is of frightening complexity — of the same complexity as in the Middle Ages and the seventeenth century.

Organized religion has the right, even the duty, to protest against any anti-religious movement or institution which threatens to influence man's conscience by means of organized propaganda or legislation. There is, of course, the undeniable fact that the various Christian churches themselves, when in power, did not hesitate to use mental pressure or the power of governments against supposed heretics, even if they were profoundly religious. Only with distress can one read today certain papal encyclicals against the heresy of democracy, or learn about the politics of German Protestantism against progressive social movements — all this not in the seventeenth, but in the nineteenth and twentieth centuries.

But sins of the past cannot prevent a person or an institution from acting in the present and caring for the future. It is exactly the lessons from history, however, which should make the representatives of religion cautious against the temptation to mix, consciously or unconsciously, vested interests with truly religious motives. Nothing has hurt religion more than mistakes of this kind. And with growing enlightenment among the populace today more than ever the clergy will be looked at with diffidence exactly by those it wants to convince if they are suspicious that there are ulterior motives behind the heroic gesture. This suspicion has split off from the established churches first the liberal and then the socialist movements of the European continent. Also in our day religious doctrine will be powerless in face of the great issues unless it dares reveal the good or the evil in whatever political or economic system it may appear.

Human institutions err even if they feel God-inspired, just as individuals sometimes mistake their merely subjective intuitions for the voice of God. Hence, wherever the principles of Christianity seem to conflict with political movements, let it never be forgotten that the study of theology or belief in a dogma creates expertship in social problems just as little as politics or the mastery of laboratory methods justifies any claim to judge complex issues of religion and philosophy.

How much clearer would the role of the churches in adult education and our whole cultural situation be if those clergymen who dare free their denominations not only from political involvements but also from old superstitions found more support among their colleagues. It is not the cult and the ritual which do harm to organized religion — on the contrary, they are necessary implements. What does harm among those who otherwise should be the leading laymen in their churches is the literal and magical rather than the symbolical interpretation of cult and dogma. There are many prayers, practices, and sermons which do not really elevate the mind of man toward the Holy, but either keep him for his whole life in a state of mental infantilism or cause him to rebel when he suddenly discovers the anthropomorphic and superstitious qualities of his early religious influences. Only if the churches combine political with intellectual integrity can they help modern man to become mature and thus remain one of the great factors in adult culture. They must not put dogma above the honest thoughts and deeds of man; they must frankly acknowledge and help to fight old economic and political evils even if they dislike radical cures and the philosophies behind them; and they must not mistake romantic insincerities for religious reverence. Man has always tested ideas not only by what they say, but by how they work.

(c) *Adult Education and Common Values.* In a discussion on adult education, we have to go beyond religion as a force in adult education into the problem of values and *Weltanschauung* in the general and secular sense of the word.

We have to ask the question: to what degree is any adult culture possible without some common relation to values which order the scattered beliefs and experiences of men into a continuous stream of meaning, though these values may not be expressed in forms of a religious tradition? There is no reason to be prejudiced against either the assertion, or the denial, of the necessity of a metaphysical foundation for moral standards. The moral record of religious believers is, in all likelihood, not better than that of serious "unbelievers." And there are just as good theoretical arguments in favor of the naturalist's assumption that the value patterns of civilized peoples are the result of accumulated experience, as there are good arguments in favor of a metaphysical conception of ethics. The terms "naturalism" and "idealism" are anyhow no longer clearly distinctive; there are naturalists with metaphysics, as there are idealists with a strong leaning toward pantheism in the sense of naturalistic monism. Perhaps it would be good for philosophy if the whole vocabulary by which professors try to organize for their students the wealth of philosophical wisdom could be abolished.

So, at the first glance, it might seem impossible to decide whether we should try to find the integration of our daily experiences merely on the level of man, as do the radical humanists, the pragmatists, or the Russian Communists with their concepts of a better society, or whether we should try to arrive at a common meaning of life by following, so to speak, a vertical direction toward a transcendent Unity.

On this question men of equal intelligence differ and even the most honest expression of each of us is bound to be subjective. So far as I can judge, the greater and more productive inspirations of man have not been mere observations and expansions of thought on the surface of society. Even the father of modern Communism, Karl Marx, had his intellectual foundation in much deeper dimensions than in economics and descriptive sociology. He was profoundly influenced by the Judeo-Christian tradition and by the idealism of Hegel. The mere fact that a man violently fights a tradition is no proof that he has not been nourished by it. Furthermore, it is one-sided to make "moral" behavior, which may well be reducible to mere social experience, the only criterion of value. In judging a civilization and its bearers, should we not apply also such categories as "courageous," "inspired," "productive"?

Then, the following question arises: Has Western man in the age of dominating anti-metaphysical empiricism shown an increase in these qualities? Has he become freer, more cultured, more profound? To be sure, larger masses have become more informed about more things, and technically more advanced, but at the same time there is a terrific lack of men who could provide fullness, direction, and inspiration for the life of the many.

With respect to creativeness in the realm of human problems, the mentality of our present "democratic" age is closer to the age of Alexandria at the end of antiquity than to that of the Victorian age. We have bigger and bigger libraries, more and more accuracy about facts, and less and less inner certainty. Science, which rests on observation and calculations, advances and gives us the most amazing clues to the understanding of the physiological side of nature and the human person and we have the marvelous discoveries of depth psychology. But in all thought that concerns man and society in their essence and totality, we are uncreative, and we act accordingly. Somehow our culture seems to be desiccating in spite of all its output, like a field from which the water has been drained off.

Certainly we should not expect the emergence of a new metaphysical system that would take all mankind into its comforting shelter and give them the feeling of complete rational unity. When did this ever happen? Old China, old India, and Greece, even before Socrates and the Sophists, knew there were differing ways to approach the mysteries in the universe and our own souls. They all had their orthodoxies, their heresies, and their relativisms. How, then, can we wait today for the doubtful blessings of uniformity when the wealth of discoveries and new logical designs sweeps over us like waves over an inexperienced swimmer?

One may nevertheless dream of a day when we have a better answer than just our shoulder-shrugging sort of tolerance for every and any opinion, a tolerance that in essence is nothing but the subdued sigh of unhappy indecisiveness. "Que sais-je?" — What do I know? — wrote Montaigne under his coat of arms. "Que sais-je?" every decent man has to ask himself day by day, especially the philosopher. In order to appreciate various scientific hypotheses and various cultures we have to believe in pluralism. Yet, is there not behind all this multitude of ideas and civilizations one uniting phenomenon: the reflective and self-reflective mind of man which not only mirrors life, but re-organizes it in ever-new concepts and images?

When we ponder even superficially about this mind and its capacity of thinking, i.e., of its capacity of relating itself with rationality to worlds near and far away, there emerges before us the greatest of all mysteries. A mystery it is because it is inexplicable, but at the same time it is the greatest of all revelations. It reveals to us that the mental universe in which we live is one of infinite transcendence. There is a continual meeting between the individual human mind and reality, a continual flow and flux, give and take, challenge and response, with all corresponding parts partaking of a greater order. Unless there existed this greater and embracing order in the connection between human reason and the cosmos, how could there be thinking that somehow can be tested? For every test, however imperfect, refers to a relationship not only between idea and idea, but also between an idea and the reality it wishes to express. How could there ever be change, for without some inherent continuity change would immediately degenerate into chaos? How, despite all uncertainty, could we look back into the past and forward into the future? How could we be "persons" retaining ourselves from infancy to old age?

The moment one is deeply penetrated by such a consciousness of the nature of man and his relation to the universe, he will be extremely tolerant in regard to almost all things pertaining to knowledge; he will deeply enjoy its ever-moving and progressing character. It makes no difference whether he forms his *Weltanschauung* as a result of systematic philosophical search, as happens only with a few, or whether he arrives at it without conscious formulation. Whoever feels the inner search will combine his reverence for the thousandfold appearances of life with a profound belief in a deeper principle behind all its plurality. In all uncertainty he will have one certainty: that man receives his stature, dignity, and freedom from his power of mental self-transcendence; that there is a brotherhood of men because they are participants in life's continual self-creation. This consciousness, on the one hand, will be the fountain of our sympathy for all that tries to live and grow with others. On the other hand, it will tell us where tolerance must have its limits lest it destroy itself.

For whenever men try to draw away from underneath humanity its consciousness of belonging to a greater order, when they destroy the ground of our rationality and our sense of the whole, then they destroy the foundation of human existence, whether they know it or not, whether they are philosophers, cynics, or tyrants. When man is denied to be man in this "trans"-physical sense he has to defend not only his individual welfare as a free citizen, but the very possibility of civilization.

If this consciousness of the essential conditions of civilization pervades our feeling, thinking and doing, then different men may prefer different ways and means of living and striving; nevertheless, there will be a sense of belonging together. Then also education for both the young and the adults will have found the source in which to root and from which to grow.

CHAPTER EIGHT

Summary

MOST AMERICANS WILL PROBABLY ACKNOWLEDGE the progress that has been achieved during the past decades in our elementary schools. Not everything is perfect in the grades; far from it. But the elementary school, as the school of younger children, represents a relatively protected domain of educational operation. Its aims are clearly definable, and both the young pupil as well as the subject matter he has to conquer are somehow within the grasp of educational theory and practice.

In contrast, the modern American high school reflects all the diversities of modern civilization, intellectually, socially, and spiritually. In the face of advanced requirements the differences in learning capacity begin to show more strongly. So do the social cleavages in our culture, for in contrast to the elementary school child, the adolescent is already more molded by and conscious of differences in the status of his parents. In addition, for by far the large majority of its students, the high school opens directly into vocational life and a wage-earning situation with its thousands of requirements and demands, successes and frustrations.

It is, therefore, unsatisfactory and dangerous from an educational and a general social point of view that despite all changes in the details of the curriculum we operate the high school as if it were still a part of the secondary school system of 1890, only enormously expanded and diluted. Nobody gains in this way. Both the intellectually as well as the practically gifted youth receive at the same time too much and too little; the first too much triviality and too little intellectualism, the second too much intellectualism and too little practical doing. Since the old apprenticeship system no longer exists, and since industry no longer needs young people, we put them into a parking place and call it school. The whole situation is much more a passive reaction to changes in our employment situation during the past two generations than an indigenous educational achievement.

All this is explainable with respect to the rapid transition of this nation from a society of farmers and artisans to an industrial society. However, we should not constantly asseverate our profound respect for democracy and at the same time fail to work out principles and practices by which to harmonize its two ideals of equality and respect for individual development. Certainly these two ideals, though not contradictory from a deeper point of view, are not easy to reconcile on the social plane. But this is no excuse that so far we have nothing but compromise.

Of course, a school should try to unite young people by means of intellectual learning as much as possible. But you will soon discover that beyond a relatively low level of academic achievement the differences in intelligence and aptitudes will block your desire for unification. Do not, then, close your eyes and try to placate your bad conscience by sentimental phrases. For fulfilling the democratic demand of equality within diversity, and for educating men and women of character, use the great educational chance that lies in the cultivation of man's emotional life. There is our deepest community. This community makes it possible for us to feel mutual sympathy and understanding before the wonders of birth and death, in our joys and sorrows, in the healthy mastery of our bodies and in sickness, and in our feelings of religious reverence before the universe of spirit and nature. But when it comes to more advanced and specialized intellectual pursuits, equally necessary for the survival of modern civilization as the cultivation of our emotions, then do not try to achieve conformity by hook or by crook, but select and articulate courageously according to individual talent and interest.

The confusion resulting from an unprincipled pursuit of the two equally democratic ideals of equality and quality has also crept into higher education. Whenever the universities were great they fulfilled three tasks: they interpreted to their contemporaries the deeper meanings and aspirations of their civilization; they trained men for character and moral leadership (the original sense of the English gentleman ideal as represented by Oxford and Cambridge); and they considered scholarship a sacred function in the service of truth (Paris and the early Berlin).

Can we really flatter ourselves that our colleges and universities still live up to these standards? Have they not also been drawn into the whirlpool of haphazard information about everything and anything that may occur under the sun? Furthermore, is not much of our popular adult education more a form of passing the time or of acquiring some isolated skill and information than a molding cultural factor in our democratic civilization? In view of what is being done in other countries, as for example in Scandinavia, but especially in the Communist nations with their ruthless system of indoctrination, can we afford to leave our working adult population more and more in the grip of the movies, television, and a rapidly deteriorating radio? Should we not try to conceive of adult education as an enterprise deeply rooted in the social and spiritual interests of a free adult?

All that has been said here is not only a matter of "education" in the isolated sense of the word. It is a matter of our political future, both national and international.

More and more, though against the older tradition of his country, the average American evaluates a person no longer according to his personal value and social contribution, but according to the length of his school attendance. To the same degree to which this nation has become bureaucratic, it also has trained itself to believe in credits, grades, school certificates, and academic titles. Nothing, however, is more unrealistic. Some of our schools give their pupils more to learn and think about in ten years than others in twelve; yet, some students learn more even in a bad school than others in a good one. Some pupils receive from their teachers the incentive for later development, others "hate" them together with all that reminds them of classrooms. If, say in Denmark, a boy at the age of eighteen graduates from the Gymnasium, he masters his mother tongue rather well; he knows, in addition, three modern and probably one or two ancient languages, and if he has not studied Latin and Greek, he has progressed rather far in the sciences and mathematics. In contrast, most of our high school students believe that even those who prepare for college do not need a foreign language. They belong to a big, rich, and powerful people, and they are told that when an English-speaking person talks English long enough, the others will understand him somehow. The question, however, remains whether he understands the others. The negative answer which reality gives to this question explains the disconcerting experience that this nation, though helpful in winning two World Wars, never profited from its victories. Rather it was given the rare privilege of financing the peace, as it had financed the war.

Our provincial concept of education is also responsible for the fact that the average American, who as a citizen participates in determining the future of the world, allows many of his daily newspapers to be offensively narrow in horizon and shallow in depth.

Yet, the United States is not only a big, but also a great country; it has risen from colonial origins to a world power, and within its boundaries lives a busy people, to which not only fugitives and immigrants, but men and women from all walks of life have come.

Is this merely the result of more land, more resources, more money, of everything's being "bigger than anywhere else"? Certainly not. It is primarily the result of an interaction between man and nature, of an enormous release of energy due to the fact that immigrants, who generally represent a human stock of strength and courage, found themselves no longer in a situation of narrowness and suppression, but in front of seemingly boundless opportunities. And, last but not least, they found themselves before the stern command of frontier life: "Work or die."

The situation of the open frontier no longer exists. Of course, the world is still potentially open, unless the curse of nationalism shuts off each country more and more from the other. Mere physical energy, the hand that can plow the field and swing the axe, even shrewdness and will to power, however, are no longer sufficient. Co-operative thinking and research of excellent quality are needed, together with national and international planning on the highest level of statesmanship. But all this intellectual progress will be useless without the pride, the skill and devotion of the farmer, the craftsman, and the industrial worker. Unless *all* these powers in the nation interact, and unless education helps *everyone* to find and fill his place, there will be no nation. In other words, mere horizontal expansion such as of the frontier days is theoretically and practically obsolete. Today the nation's energy has to be channeled and disciplined according to meaningful and realistic purposes; depth and form must be added to width.

But those who determine our educational policy still act as if expansion and prolongation were still the main purpose of the American school system, as it was a hundred or fifty years ago. They plan the future of this nation and the whole world, but actually they live in the past. For example, the *Report of the President's Commission on Higher Education* believes that in 1960 a minimum of 4,600,000 young people should be enrolled in non-profit institutions for education beyond the traditional twelfth grade. (At present about 2,400,000 students are enrolled in colleges.) But what is going to happen to all these students? Will they still have the boundaries of life open? Yes, the best of them will, because the productive and courageous do not depend on given material conditions; they make new productive agreements with life, not only for themselves, but also for their fellow men. Also, human society will always look for professional people of high quality.

But it is false to believe that prolonged schooling as such will be rewarded in the future. If we send more and more youth, whether or not they like it, into primarily verbal schools, no longer for eight or ten years, but for twelve, and perhaps for fourteen, we will *not* create more education, more initiative, more happiness, more democracy, and more integration within this nation.

One may say that the more somebody has learned, the better it is for him. That is true provided he has learned something in line with his later life; if it is contrary to it, he becomes bewildered and frustrated. A man is happy in his occupation only if it somehow materializes that which he has hoped and worked for during the years of preparation. If the expectancies built up during his education remain unfulfilled, if, in concrete terms, he finally becomes a mechanic rather than an engineer as he dreamed of, he probably will not be a good and happy mechanic, who, as such, is a very useful person.

Certainly, the chance which a free society gives a person involves risk. Yet, it would be a tragic misunderstanding of the great concepts of freedom, equality, and democracy if our youth were buoyed up with illusions about a sort of life that does not exist, so that they become disenchanted the moment they meet the stern facts of reality. In other words, educational ideologists who believe that schools as such are instruments strong enough to neglect without punishment the psychological, economic, and political conditions of society, will not help in improving their society and in making the ideals of democracy more and more real. Rather they will create first confusion, and then some kind of tyranny for "restoring order." For, what Francis Bacon says of man's relation to nature holds true also with respect to his relation to society:

Man, as the minister and interpreter of nature, does and understands as much as his observations on the order of nature, either with regard to things or the mind, permit him, and neither knows nor is capable of more.

These words should not be understood in the sense that education be considered nothing but an adjunct to economics and politics. Education has the power to change society gradually. But though faith in ideals is the greatest force of progress, only that faith and those ideals can achieve the goal which are in congruence with, and not against, the laws of nature and of mental and social development.

Whether she wants or not, the United States of America has been given a leading role in the political and economic re-organization of the world. This role will not be finished when our children are adults. If they do not become ready for it, intellectually as well as in terms of a strong inner discipline — more ready than we were — they will fail. A man can lead or remain in leadership only with a strong sense of orientation. In addition, he must be able constantly to test his means and ends by ever-widening criteria of thought and action. Such capacities are not just a gift from heaven, or the result of quick information. For the fulfillment of great duties and decisions, man must be forearmed already in an early age through directed living and learning.

This book has been written in the hope that it may help parents and teachers to provide for our youth, and also for our adults, an educational atmosphere where such directed living and learning is possible.

Index

230